AN INTRODUCTION TO

ARCHÆOLOGY

AN INTRODUCTION TO

ARCHÆOLOGY

A QUANTUM BOOK

Published by Shooting Star Press, Inc.
230 Fifth Avenue, Suite 1212
New York, NY 10001
USA

ISBN 1-57335-477-5

This book was produced by
Quantum Books Ltd
6 Blundell Street
London N7 9BH

Printed in China by Leefung-Asco Printers Ltd

CONTENTS

WHAT IS ARCHAEOLOGY?

ABOVE The Roman triumphal arch at the end of the main colonnaded street at Palmyra in Syria, an important caravan city in Roman times.

■ THE MEANING OF ARCHAEOLOGY

When people think of archaeology, they tend to think of excavations, particularly those in distant lands such as Egypt and Greece. They might think of glass-cased collections of curios, but they rarely think about the old house next door, the ridges and mounds in the field down the road, or the bits of old pottery that they dig up in the garden. Yet archaeology includes all of these.

Archaeology is often considered as a branch of history, and to some extent this is true. History is the study of the past using documents and inscriptions as evidence, and historians have recorded and interpreted events from the earliest days of writing up to the present day. Archaeology, on the other hand, is the study of the past using objects and other excavated evidence as the main source of data. This allows the study of peoples without any form of writing, as well as of literate civilizations. Almost anything can be used to shed light on the past: the foundations of buildings can show what sort of houses people lived in; the remains of tools show how they worked; animal bones and plant remains show what they ate; and pollen, snail shells and the remains of trees and plants can indicate the type of climate and vegetation at the time. What archaeology cannot do is tell us the names of the people and what great deeds they did, how they influenced each other, and what they thought and believed in – these are things that only historical evidence can tell us.

Archaeologists and historians studying the period since writing has been in use – the last few thousand years – examine different types of evidence, although they overlap at many points. For example, a historian will be interested in finding out what is written on a sheet of medieval vellum, whereas an archaeologist will want to know what animal skin was used, how the vellum was made, and what pigments were used for

BELOW Excavations in distant countries with hot climates is the popular idea of archaeology. This excavation is taking place at Tell Akko (Acre) in Israel, an important biblical port. This particular part of the excavations is concentrating on the Bronze Age and Iron Age levels.

the ink. Since the first use of writing, historical and archaeological sources of evidence have enabled a much more complete picture of the past to be compiled. The period of human history before writing, however, known as *prehistory*, lasted for hundreds of thousands of years. For the majority of human existence, therefore, only archaeological evidence can give clues about the past.

Because archaeology uses many types of material remains as evidence, supplementing them with historical evidence wherever possible, the subject of archaeology overlaps just about every other academic discipline. For example, archaeologists collaborate with petrologists in studying the rocks from which tools were made, with biologists in studying plant and animal remains, with physicians in studying the diseases from which people suffered, and with physicists for complex dating methods. Furthermore, the many branches of archaeology are wide-ranging, including prehistory (the study of humankind before the advent of writing), historical archaeology (the study of humankind in the historical period), and garden history which studies upstanding and buried monuments as well as documents in order to research old landscape gardens. Archaeology does not just deal with buried evidence, but also with sites and objects of all kinds; the study of buildings is considered equally important. Industrial archaeology, for example, involves the investigation, surveying, recording and preservation of old industrial buildings, and also of all associated equipment and machinery of all kinds. In an age where many people specialize in their work lives, it is the rounded, all-embracing nature of archaeology that makes it such a fascinating and popular pursuit.

THE EARLY DAYS OF ARCHAEOLOGY

The contemporary interest in period costume drama (a medieval film will usually show knights in armour, the servants in tunics and tights; a performance of William Shakespeare's *Julius Caesar* might well dress the men in togas) is a

relatively recent phenomenon. In Shakespeare's time, *Julius Caesar* and other plays with a historical background were performed in what was then modern dress (what we would recognize as Elizabethan costume). This was not an avant-garde approach to theatre, but at that time, and in the preceding medieval period, people had no concept of the past being significantly different from the present. With little idea of measurement backwards in time, the past was like a box in which all earlier times were jumbled together. Consequently, Julius Caesar was dressed in Elizabethan costume because no one thought that he ought to be dressed any differently.

ABOVE Archaeology involves a broad range of activities and studies. Even on excavations, a large variety of tasks have to be done. Here, the draughts-person is drawing a scale plan of an Anglo-Saxon cremation urn.

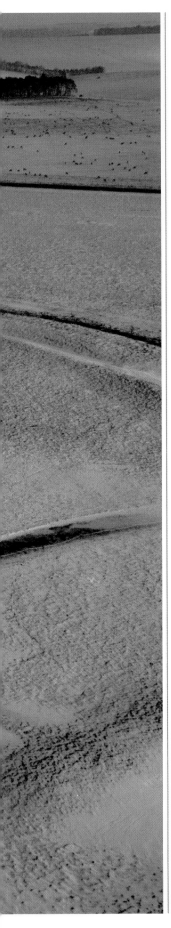

FAR LEFT An aerial view of the prehistoric monument of Stonehenge, England, with snow highlighting not just the stones, but some of the many associated earthworks.

LEFT A 14th century manuscript depicting the medieval legend that the magician Merlin was responsible for erecting the lintels at Stonehenge.

As well as this two-dimensional view, people also had relatively little curiosity about the past. Although many more ancient monuments and ruins existed than survive today, they were either thought of as relatively recent ruins or natural phenomena, or else they were explained away as having been made by gods or legendary heroes. Because of these beliefs, many archaeological sites today still bear legendary names such as King Arthur's Cave, Devil's Dyke or Giant's Grave. One of the few exceptions to this was Stonehenge, which always seems to have been regarded as extremely old and to have excited theories about how the lintels were raised: one early theory was that the magician Merlin placed the stones.

This lack of curiosity about the past was probably largely caused by the fact that the Bible was accepted as a complete account of the beginning of the world and its early history, a view that was not seriously challenged until the late 19th century. Until then, it was thought that the date

of creation was fairly recent and was certainly not earlier than 5,000BC.

Before the 16th century, virtually the only people concerned with the past were the medieval chroniclers who relied on written records and oral traditions. One exception was the scholar Cyriac of Ancona (*b.* 1391) who spent 25 years in Greece, visiting sites and libraries, and making observations. In this direct recording of physical remains, Cyriac was a pioneer of the methods of the early topographers of the 16th century onwards.

Archaeology is usually regarded as having its beginnings in the mid 16th century with the work of topographers such as John Leland (1506–1552) who was employed by Henry VIII as 'Keeper of King's Libraries' and so travelled extensively. He made an inventory of monuments and recorded the history of the places he visited. Although his work was not published, his idea of recording physical remains as part of a wider study of the landscape foreshadowed the work

RIGHT A typical view of a 19th century excavation, of the Anglo-Saxon burial mound at Taplow. It was excavated in an unsystematic way, and the many illustrations of finds show that the emphasis was put on the recovered finds rather than on the site itself. In this illustration, published soon after the excavation in 1883, the burial was attributed to the Vikings.

The original caption read: 'A Viking's Tomb, Lately Discovered at Taplow Court, near Maidenhead. 1. Relative positions of the Mound and the Manor House, Taplow Court. 2. The Excavation, Grave at A, 30ft from surface. 3. The Old Yew-tree, in 1882, from photograph by Mr. J. Rutland. 4. Silver Armlet found in the Grave. 5. Gold Band. 6. Gold Wristlet. 7. Gold Waist Buckle. 8. Gold Buckle. 9. Part of Bucket. 10. Ornaments from Shield. 11, 13, 14. British Pottery. 12. Samian Ware. 15. Part of Drinking Horn.'

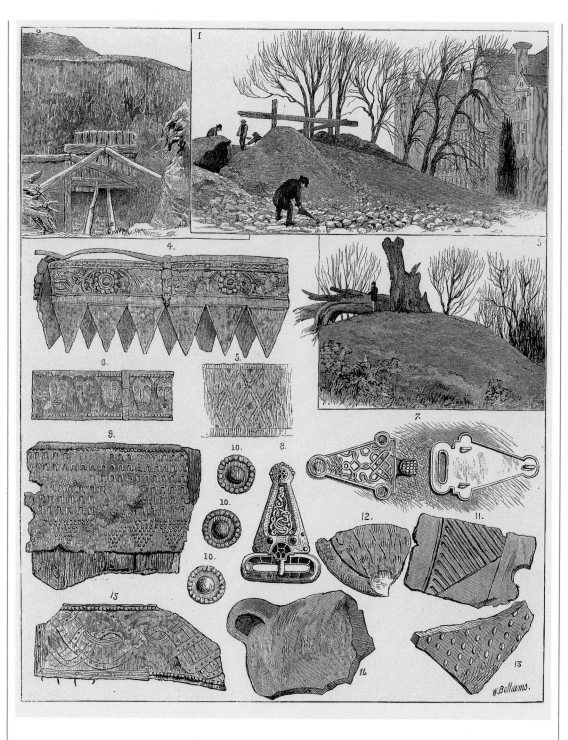

of later topographers such as William Camden (1551–1623).

By the end of the century, there was a growing feeling that finds and monuments belonged to a past that ought to be recorded, and around 1585 William Camden wrote his book *Brittania*. The original version was in Latin but later editions were in English, and numerous reprints were published up until the early 18th century. This was the first book to give topo-graphical descriptions of monuments in Britain, with reference to manuscripts, monuments and finds, and was a model that many similar works followed up until the early 19th century. The influence of works such as *Brittania* led to the creation of private collections, and so to the formation of private museums.

The foundations of modern archaeology were laid down in the 17th century, and throughout the 17th and 18th centuries emphasis was put on the recording of archaeological monuments, initially as part of general topographical works, but eventually as part of a study of the monuments themselves. Scholars like John Aubrey (1626–1697) became interested in the information they were collecting for its own sake, and not simply as evidence gathered to prove a particular point of view. Despite the fact that Aubrey's topographical manuscript *Monumenta Britannica* was not published in his own lifetime (although parts have been published subsequently), the manuscript greatly influenced William Stukeley (1687–1765) who carried out extensive fieldwork, particularly in southern England.

The 18th-century interest in antiquities was also due in part to the fashion of touring European countries – the 'Grand Tour'. Such travellers inevitably brought home souvenirs, many of which were antiquities, and the sight of the classical remains in Greece and Italy prompted some travellers to investigate the history of their own countries.

By the end of the 18th century, however, the emphasis was beginning to change from fieldwork to excavation. Many people were no longer content to record ancient monuments: they wanted to know more about them and, in particular, they wanted objects for their private museums. To meet these needs, most excavations were concentrated on burial mounds, as these offered the best chance of recovering complete objects worthy of display; in the early and mid 19th century, the recovery of objects was the primary reason for excavation.

This situation only started to change in the late 19th century as more excavators tried to understand what they were finding. Excavations such as those of the German excavator Heinrich Schliemann (1822–90) at Troy and Mycenae, of the British archaeologist Arthur Evans (1851–1951) at Knossos, and of many others at this time began to prove that much more than objects for display in a museum could be recovered from these sites.

The way forward was shown by General Pitt-Rivers (1827–1900). After a career in the British army, during which time he had done a great deal of fieldwork and excavation, and had amassed a collection of artefacts from all over the world, he spent the rest of his life studying and

excavating archaeological sites on his estate. He conducted research into how artefacts gradually develop over a period of time, the study of which is known as typology. He also carried out archaeological experiments, and was the first Inspector of Ancient Monuments in Great Britain, appointed in 1883. It was Pitt-Rivers' methods of excavation, though, that were his most important contribution to archaeology. He laid the foundations of modern excavation practice, laying emphasis on the

ABOVE A painting of General Pitt-Rivers (1827–1900), a pioneer of the techniques of archaeological excavation.

importance of controlled dissection of sites to gather information, rather than undisciplined digging to uncover buried buildings and finds. Pitt-Rivers was well aware that excavation destroys evidence as it uncovers it, and so he kept meticulous records. Furthermore, he published the results of his excavations fully in the four volumes of *Excavations in Cranborne Chase,* which have been a model for subsequent excavation reports.

The principles of excavation that Pitt-Rivers pioneered were slow to be adopted. In particular, the importance of stratigraphy and the need to examine the structure of the site as a whole was rarely appreciated. Sir Mortimer Wheeler (1890–1976) excavated many sites, particularly in Great Britain and on the Indian subcontinent. He greatly influenced modern methods of excavation: he deliberately studied Pitt-Rivers' methods and modified them to his own ideas. In 1954 he published *Archaeology from the Earth,* an instruction book on field archaeology; many modern excavation techniques have their origins in the principles that Wheeler set out in that book. He was one of the pioneers in opening up archaeology to everyone, both through his books and through radio and television appearances.

The importance of landscape survey as the primary source of archaeological evidence was eclipsed by excavation at the end of the 18th century, and never fully recovered. But the use of aircraft in the First World War showed the potential of aerial reconnaissance for discovering and interpreting archaeological sites, and this technique was pioneered by OGS Crawford (1886–1957). As a result, interest in non-destructive fieldwork was rekindled and continues today alongside excavation.

Indeed, since the First World War, the development of archaeology has accelerated dramatically. Advances in methods of excavation have been accompanied by various electronic devices for locating sites, more accurate methods of dating, and perhaps most important of all, many sophisticated techniques for interpreting the evidence provided by excavation and landscape survey, so that our understanding of the past has improved dramatically. Many of these aspects are looked at in the following chapters.

WHO DOES ARCHAEOLOGY?

In the early days of archaeology, the dividing line between archaeologists and treasure hunters was all but invisible. Such was the general level of knowledge, that it was easily possible for a treasure hunter to know more about the subject than someone claiming to be an archaeologist. Today, the gap between treasure hunters and archaeologists is considerable, and there is little possibility of confusing the two: the main aim of the treasure hunter is to make a financial gain from what is found, whereas the main aim of the archaeologist is to investigate the past.

The three main types of people who practise archaeology are professional archaeologists, amateur enthusiasts, and students, although this varies from country to country. Some countries have a state archaeological service run entirely by professional field archaeologists, so that amateurs, and sometimes even archaeological students are not allowed to participate in field-work or excavation. At the other end of the spectrum, some countries have hardly any professional archaeologists, and even these may be confined to looking after museum collections.

The idea of full-time professional archaeologists is relatively new. Before the Second World War, virtually the only people able to practise archaeology on a full-time basis were those employed in museums, or the few who had sufficient wealth to be self-financing. Very few universities had departments of archaeology, there were fewer museums and museum staff than there are nowadays, and overall there were far fewer full-time archaeologists.

BELOW An archaeological excavation being run by full-time professional field archaeologists based in a university. Here a group of visitors is being shown a Roman tile kiln.

LEFT Sir Mortimer Wheeler (1890–1976) achieved outstanding success as an excavator in Britain and on the Indian subcontinent. He was also a radio and television broadcaster.

LEFT Computers and other electronic devices are now essential tools in archaeology for handling the vast amounts of data that fieldwork produces.

ABOVE The study of human remains can yield much information about a past society – diet, life expectancy, diseases, and so on. Sometimes bodies are preserved through mummification or in waterlogged deposits, but more often only skeletons survive.

Professional archaeologists themselves can be divided into three principal groups: field archaeologists, university archaeologists, and museum archaeologists. Field archaeologists tend to specialize in fieldwork and excavation and are particularly involved with the practical aspects of archaeology, whereas university archaeologists are usually concerned with teaching students of archaeology and conducting archaeological research, often based on the results of the work of field archaeology. In the main, museum archaeologists are concerned with the study of the archaeological collections in their care. However, the divisions betwen these groups of archaeologists are seldom this clear-cut. For example, an archaeologist in a museum attached to a university may also lecture to students, as well as direct research excavations for the university, and thus perform many of the functions of all three types of professional archaeologist.

Museum archaeologists and field archaeologists are usually employed to undertake work in a specific locality within their own country,

whereas university archaeologists are often able to undertake fieldwork and excavations in other countries, which is particularly useful for countries which have very few archaeologists of their own.

In some countries, there are thriving societies of amateur archaeologists, usually composed of people who are enthusiastically interested in the subject, and devote much of their leisure time to it, despite having no formal training or professional qualifications. In places where no professional archaeologists operate, amateurs fill an important gap, but more frequently they work alongside, and co-operate with, the professional archaeologists in their area.

Amateur societies vary greatly in their activities. Some are very much involved in field archaeology and publications, while others concentrate on organizing excursions to sites and museums for their members, and most provide an annual programme of lectures. Although the overwhelming majority of the members are amateurs, many professional archaeologists belong to at least one society, and some have a high proportion of professional members.

University students of all kinds, not just those studying archaeology, often participate in excavations in vacations, and some university archaeology departments require their students to do a certain amount of practical work, on site or in a museum, as part of their course work. Extra-mural students often get involved in practical archaeological work as well, and are particularly useful in undertaking fieldwork projects in their own locality.

Although in some countries participation in practical work is restricted (because of employment regulations, for example), in most places it is possible for anyone to become involved in some aspect of archaeology.

■ WHY DO ARCHAEOLOGY?

In an age where commercial profit and gain are predominant, the purpose of archaeology is often called into question. The main reason for pursuing archaeology is, of course, to find out as much as possible about how recent and remote societies lived and operated. This desire to discover can take several different forms, depending on a person's range of knowledge. For most people though there is a curiosity about the past, about how people lived and behaved, about whether they have changed over the centuries, and this can in part be answered by archaeology. The good preservation of bodies, either deliberately (mummification) or accidentally (as with bodies preserved in peat bogs), often gives a good idea of what people actually looked like in previous times. The remains of houses and possessions give an idea of people's lifestyle, while the remains of their tools can show what work they did, and to some extent how hard they would have had to work to do a particular job.

Environmental evidence can also give wide-ranging information on past environments and climates.

Questions concerning landscape features and ancient monuments – what they are, how old they are, who made them, and so on – can in part be answered by archaeological evidence, and

LEFT Through archaeology it is possible to find out many details about ancient settlements, so that houses and the general landscape can be reconstructed fairly accurately. This is a reconstruction of an Iron Age farm at Butser, England.

ABOVE TOP The spectacular 1st century AD Roman theatre at Jerash in Jordan is a popular tourist attraction.

in the case of prehistoric monuments, it is the only means available of deducing such information.

This interest in what is often termed 'cultural heritage' also involves other studies, such as local history, heraldry and genealogy, but archaeology has an active role to play in providing a coherent picture of our heritage. Many mis-

conceptions about the past have already been corrected, and in all likelihood many more will only be put right through continued archaeological research. For example, it is still commonplace in cartoons to show cavemen and dinosaurs together, despite the fact that it has been known for many years that dinosaurs were extinct long before the evolution of 'cavemen'. Similarly, early humans are always portrayed as hunters, surviving largely on a diet of meat, and this interpretation is still being taught to schoolchildren. However, current research shows that early humans did not generally rely on a meat diet, but that plant foods were at least as important: far from being mighty hunters, early humans are more likely to have been opportunist scavengers. Part of the misconception arose because the bones of early humans have often been found with bones of other animals, and it was simplistically assumed that this showed that they had killed and eaten other animals, and had later died amid the remains of previous meals. Recent research has

shown that in such cases it is more likely that the animals and humans had been eaten by other predators, such as leopards an hyenas.

In many countries, one practical offshoot of the growth of interest in the heritage is the growth of tourism. Most tourist sights are sites of historical or archaeological importance, and archaeology has an expanding role in the presentation of such attractions. Historical sites and ancient monuments that are badly presented, providing little or no explanation, seldom achieve popularity as tourist sites unless they are unique and already world-famous, as in the case of Stonehenge, in Wiltshire. Consequently, many sites have benefited from archaeological research, and in some cases excavation, in order to be properly presented to the visitors.

In the modern industrial world, more and more people are feeling a need to find out about their immediate and distant past, and this is likely to increase in the future. This enhances the moral duty for archaeologists to rescue as much infor-

mation as possible about the past before it is destroyed. Future generations are likely to deplore the way current societies are allowing so much of their heritage to be destroyed without record. A society that ignores its past deserves to have no future.

Perhaps the most important and least obvious reason for doing archaeology is that, in many ways, the past is the key to the present and to the future. Archaeology helps us to understand the past, and this understanding helps a great deal in the understanding of society today and the development of society in the future. An explorer who does not compile maps as he or she proceeds is likely to end up going round in circles; likewise, a society that does not know where it has come from in the past has no chance of knowing where it is going in the future. In this way, archaeology is central to all knowledge, which is why it appeals to so many different people. Archaeology has, quite literally, something for everyone.

ABOVE Part of the huge 6th century AD mosaic found at Madaba in Jordan showing the earliest known view of Jerusalem. Early maps exist to show how people conceived of the world at the time, but unless made of durable material, like this mosaic, such maps have not survived.

OPPOSITE PAGE, BOTTOM PHOTOGRAPH There is in fact no evidence to suggest that the Druids existed when Stonehenge was first constructed, yet modern-day Druidic cults still seek to worship there.

ANCIENT LANDSCAPES

ABOVE The commercial extraction of peat in the Somerset Levels, England, has been responsible for both the discovery and destruction of waterlogged prehistoric sites.

■ HOW ARCHAEOLOGICAL SITES BECOME BURIED

While some archaeological sites, such as the spectacular ruins at Petra in Jordan or the monolithic statues on Easter Island in the Pacific, have never been completely buried, the majority of archaeological sites and finds have to be unearthed. How sites and finds come to be buried depends on a number of factors, and there is often more than one reason why they are now beneath the ground.

The most simple reason for something being buried is that people have buried it, and domestic waste is probably the most common example of deliberate burial. On archaeological sites, pits are frequently found that were used for the disposal of household refuse that would nowadays be put in a dustbin, collected by the municipal authorities, and taken to a communal

rubbish tip. Rubbish tips nowadays often consist of large holes in the ground (such as disused quarries) which are being filled in, and which are gigantic versions of the rubbish pits found on archaeological sites. When rubbish pits are excavated, sherds of pottery and fragments of bone are frequently the only visible remains, because much of the refuse put into pits was the remnants of food preparation which have since decayed. However, microscopic analysis of the soil in a pit can sometimes show what sort of food remains were originally buried.

Burials of human and animals (corpses and cremations) are another instance of deliberate burial. In many cultures, various objects, termed grave goods, were commonly deposited with human burials. These grave goods could include one or more pots or containers, weapons, tools, and jewellery. In some cases, these may represent the personal belongings of the dead person, but many of the grave goods, such as food and coins, seem to have been buried for the benefit

BELOW The temple of Sounion in Greece is an example of a site which has never been buried. The remains have always been visible, even though the temple was erected some 2,500 years ago.

LEFT Much archaeological evidence has been deliberately buried, such as this skeleton. Bodies which were buried with their legs bent in this way are termed crouched inhumations. The draughts-person is recording the precise details and position of the bones before they are excavated.

of the dead person in the after-life. Some burials, like those of the rulers of ancient Egypt, have many grave goods.

Another common form of deliberate burial is that of a hoard of objects, such as coins, scrap metal or jewellery. Before banks or even locks and keys were invented, the usual way of protecting valuable objects and money was to hide them from other people. Often such valuables were hidden in the ground, sometimes contained in a bag, wooden chest or pot. If they were not retrieved, such hoards remained hidden until accidentally found, often hundreds or even thousands of years later. Not all hoards were meant to be recovered: some were deliberately buried as religious offerings and sacrifices. It can

RIGHT The collapse, levelling and rebuilding of mud brick houses has led to the formation of huge mounds in some parts of the world. In the Near East they are known as tells, such as this one being excavated at Tell Akko (Acre) in Israel.

RIGHT A view of Tel Megiddo in Israel looming above the landscape shows the size of tells that formed in the Near East through continuous habitation of the site.

BELOW Stone walls were often used as field boundaries, but when they are no longer maintained and collapse, they can quickly become overgrown with vegetation and hidden from view.

be very difficult to be sure of why a hoard of objects was buried in the ground.

Natural catastrophes, such as volcanic eruptions, may result in sites being buried very rapidly. The most famous example is the burial of the Roman towns of Pompeii and Herculaneum in Italy by an eruption of Vesuvius in AD 79. Other sites have also been discovered buried in ash and lava from volcanoes, and many more probably await discovery. The burial of sites by volcanic eruptions happens without warning, so that such sites are like very well-preserved time capsules. Other natural phenomena also can bury a site, including sandstorms and landslides.

In towns and cities which are occupied for long periods of time, there is a continuous process of old buildings being demolished and levelled for the construction of new ones, which in turn become old and are demolished. This process of demolition and construction gradually leads to the ground level of the whole town being raised. Resurfacing of roads and yards outside buildings adds to this process. It can be difficult to appreciate the amount by which the ground surface has been raised in this way. In the Near East, the constant rebuilding of mud brick houses has resulted in the formation of considerable mounds known as tells; the one at Jericho is over 15 metres high. This means that the evidence for early occupation is often quite deeply buried.

RIGHT This building was once a small stone cottage, but its decay and collapse has been accelerated by trees and other vegetation which have found the old building an ideal environment.

BELOW As a stone or brick building collapses, the building debris falls either side of the collapsing walls, so that the site becomes a heap of rubble, unrecognisable until it is excavated.

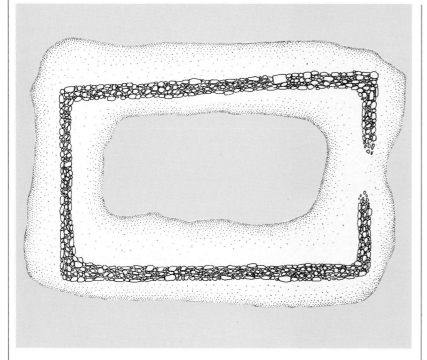

The most common, but least obvious, way that sites get buried is through the natural processes of decay and renewal. When a masonry building is abandoned and is no longer repaired, dampness within the building encourages insects and fungi to attack the timbers, while wind, rain, and changes of temperature attack the exterior of the building. Once a breach is made in the fabric of the roof – when thatch rots or slates or tiles slip – rain gets in and the processes of decay accelerate until the roof collapses. Internal walls and floors collapse and the decaying remains of their timbers become mixed with dust, leaves and other debris blown into the building to form a soil in which plants and even trees will grow. The masonry shell of the building forms a trap for more wind-blown leaves, dust and seeds, forming a deeper soil, while the weather, insects and plants attack the remaining walls from both sides. Gradually the walls collapse, a process often accelerated by the penetration of plant and tree roots between the stones. Sometimes walls are deliberately demolished so that the stone can be re-used elsewhere.

Eventually the cycle of decaying timbers, mortar and plants followed by renewed plant growth reduces the site of the building to a low mound. Even without demolition of walls, it may take only 20–30 years for a masonry building to disappear beneath the ground, but less substantial buildings can disappear even faster. Timber buildings may simply rot and collapse, and other features such as pits and ditches will silt up very rapidly once they cease to be maintained.

However, burial processes can be quite complex. For example, a Roman burial alongside a road leading from a Roman town may originally have been deliberately buried, but as the town expanded and the burial was forgotten, a house might be built over the site. In time, the house might decay, the town disappear, and the whole site become a field growing crops. It is this sort of sequence of events that archaeologists attempt to unravel when trying to understand how sites and finds have become buried.

HOW SITES ARE DESTROYED

Archaeological sites are often described as a 'diminishing non-renewable resource'. A field of rare flowers that is destroyed can be replanted and may eventually be the same as the field that was destroyed (even if the process does take 1,000 years). But each archaeological site is unique, and once destroyed, it cannot be replaced: the information it contained is lost not for 1,000 years or so, but forever.

The natural processes of decay and erosion are gradually destroying all archaeological sites. However such processes of decay take thousands or hundreds of thousands of years, wheres the main threats are much more rapid and immediate. This process is not of concern to archaeologists alone: the destruction of archaeological sites often coincides with the destruction of wildlife habitats and changes in the environment.

One of the main causes of destruction of archaeological sites is the construction of housing, industrial sites, and roads. In the past, such building work has not always been completely destructive, but modern techniques of construction usually require deep foundations, totally destroying any underlying sites. Similarly, the massive movement of earth involved in modern

BELOW When even substantial timber buildings decay and collapse, the only evidence that is usually available for archaeologists to discover are non-organic finds, and holes in the ground in which the timber posts may have been originally placed.

road construction provides little chance of survival for any archaeological site on the line of a new road; the construction of dams usually involves earth-moving on a vast scale, and the destruction and drowning of large areas of the landscape.

Mineral extraction by quarrying and open-cast mining also disturbs sites. Of the various types of mineral extraction, the exploitation of river gravels tends to be the most devastating because in the past river gravels have provided the most attractive environments for settlement, offering fertile soils and an abundant water supply. It is therefore usually the case that even more archaeological sites are destroyed on river gravels than on the hilly or mountainous ground where stone is generally quarried.

The most widespread and probably the most serious destruction of archaeological sites, though, is caused by agriculture, including ploughing, deforestation and afforestation, and drainage and clearance of marginal land. Older methods of farming only caused surface damage to archaeological sites by ploughing, but modern intensive farming destroys sites much more quickly. Particularly harmful is the process of deep ploughing, which destroys far more of an

archaeological site than the older, shallower ploughs. Moreover, the use of larger, heavier machinery necessitates the removal of obstacles, such as burial mounds and ancient field boundaries, to improve efficiency. In some countries, marginal land that was previously heath or moorland, as well as much pasture land, has been recently ploughed for the first time in centuries, with the resulting destruction of many archaeological sites.

One branch of agriculture is particularly destructive of archaeological sites: forestry. The

ABOVE The destruction of large tracts of the landscape for modern road building often involves the destruction of archaeological sites.

RIGHT An urban site being excavated before it is destroyed by the very deep foundations of modern buildings.

LEFT The construction of dams inevitably involves the destruction and submergence of archaeological sites. Here a Bronze Age site at Tel Halawa in northern Syria is being excavated in advance of flood-waters from a dam being constructed on the Euphrates.

ABOVE The preparation of land for forestry can destroy even well-preserved archaeological sites, particularly on land which has only been used for pasture. The planting, growing and felling of the trees and the use of heavy machinery adds to the destruction process.

modern methods of planting trees usually involve large amounts of banking and ditching of the plantation ground in order to provide good drainage. Any archaeological sites not destroyed in this process are likely to be at least as severely damaged by the roots of the trees, which are usually set as close together as is economically viable.

In other regions, widespread destruction of marshes and peatbogs is taking place, through drainage for improved agriculture and for reclamation purposes, and through commercial exploitation of the peat. The laying of land drains is destructive in itself, as is the deep ploughing that often follows it, but drainage also has a direct dramatic effect on archaeological sites. Water-logging of archaeological sites inhibits bacterial decay so that organic material such as wood, leather and even 'bog bodies' can survive for thousands of years – sometimes complete villages and landscapes are preserved. Once land is drained, this protection is removed from any underlying archaeological sites, and organic re-

mains begin to decay and disintegrate extremely rapidly. One example is in Florida, where peat deposits cover 3 million acres, much of which is now being systematically lost through drainage operations; hundreds of archaeological sites and finds have been destroyed with virtually no record being made.

Sites are also being destroyed in various countries by the plundering of suitable sites for finds to sell to tourists or to supply the illegal trade in saleable antiquities.

The result of the widespread destruction of archaeological sites is that most excavations have to be conducted on sites that are under threat of destruction. In fact, most archaeological sites are destroyed without any record because the pace of destruction is too great for the limited resources available to archaeologists. Nowadays, very few excavations take place on sites that do not have some form of threat of damage or destruction, because enough funds are not available to finance a full research excavation on every possible site.

LEFT Even sites deliberately set aside are in danger from agriculture and forestry, as the erosion of this burial ground by heavy machinery demonstrates.

HOW SITES ARE DISCOVERED

The most obvious way of discovering archaeological sites is to go out and look for them – but this is not quite as simple as it might seem. Numerous archaeological sites are already known and have been recorded (although often not investigated in any detail), so the first task is to find out what these sites are. This may simply involve consulting an index of all the sites, finds and monuments in the area, but if such an index does not exist, extensive research in museums and libraries may be necessary to compile such an index before any work in the field takes place.

In areas where the population is relatively small and thinly-spread, fieldworkers looking for new sites may well discover ruins and large monuments, such as burial mounds, hillforts, and rock paintings that were previously unknown. In many parts of the world, virtually no searching for sites and finds has taken place, and the poten-

tial for discovery is enormous. For example, it is thought that in Zimbabwe there are probably tens of thousands of sites of rock art, but only a tiny fraction have ever been recorded; and in Israel recent surveys have revealed thousands of previously unknown sites.

In densely populated areas, the chances of finding such obvious sites that have been overlooked by previous archaeologists are very small. In these populated areas, fieldworkers concentrate instead on looking for scatters of finds, such as sherds of pottery and worked stones, because these give an indication of where previously unknown archaeological sites lie buried: the finds are usually brought to the surface as the sites are damaged by ploughing. This process of searching for finds is called field-walking, or surface collection, and to be most effective it is done systematically. Having obtained permission to walk over the land, a group of people divide the area between them (usually in the squares of a grid marked out in some way on the ground), and each person collects and records any finds in their particular area. By plotting each spot where finds were collected on a plan, concentrations of finds will be revealed, and these may indicate the source of the finds (the archaeological site). It is necessary to look for concentrations of finds because a handful of finds could have got onto the land in any number of ways and is not necessarily an indication of the presence of a nearby archaeological site. For example, domestic waste (which could include broken pottery) was often spread on fields during manuring – the farm from which the pottery came could be some distance away. In areas where there are vast scatters of finds lying on the surface, it is not practical to collect the finds, but instead the position of the finds are accurately plotted.

Archaeological sites are often discovered by accident. Many such sites have been found during the construction of buildings, roads, railways, dams, and so on, as well as during mineral extraction. Unfortunately, such discovery is often

BELOW The systematic searching for new sites and surface finds can take place over many different terrains, often to find out more about a landscape before it is destroyed. Fieldwalking is here taking place on the mountains of Gubbio, Italy.

LEFT The destruction of sites through drainage for agricultural land improvement continues to be carried out, despite the surpluses of crops produced by many countries. Once a site is put back into production, it may not be immediately obvious that the archaeological sites have been destroyed.

RIGHT Sites and finds can often be discovered during construction work. All the archaeologist can do on the line of this new road is to hurriedly record features and salvage finds.

LEFT Through aerial photography it is easier to understand even well-documented and visible sites. This is a Neolithic henge monument in Cumbria, England. The earthworks are clearly visible, and the site can be seen to have been partly destroyed by the modern roads.

When looking for new sites on the ground, it can be very easy to overlook features or fail to understand them, whereas sites viewed from the air can be seen in their entirety.
RIGHT The site of an Iron Age broch in Scotland seen from the ground.
BELOW The same site from the air, and a much clearer picture emerges.

of limited value, since by the time the site is recognized and reported, it is usually more than half destroyed: in most cases, there is little time for archaeologists to salvage information from what is left of the site. Because of this, attempts are made in many areas to examine land destined for construction work or mineral extraction before the work starts and, if possible, to record and even excavate sites threatened with destruction. It is also useful to have an archaeologist examine the area while construction work is going on since archaeological remains are not always easily recognized by those concerned with construction.

However, the most efficient and productive method of finding archaeological sites is through aerial photography, since from the air it is possible to see sites which are difficult to recognize from ground level. Walking amongst the ruins of an ancient city, for example, it is impossible to gain an overall impression of the layout. But if a person climbs a nearby hill and looks down on the site, the whole city can be seen and to some extent understood: viewing a site at an angle in this way is equivalent to an oblique aerial photograph. If the person flies immediately above the centre of the city, the whole city is clearly displayed and comprehensible.

Oblique aerial photographs are easier to take than vertical ones, but are difficult to use afterwards, as there is distortion of the image. Vertical aerial photographs, taken from directly above a site, are used mainly for plotting features on to maps as they show less distortion. Nowadays, most maps are made by plotting features from vertical aerial photographs, using computers to correct the distortion in the photographs.

Aerial photography is particularly valuable in detecting buried archaeological sites, picking up three main clues visible from the air: marks in growing crops, marks in the soil, and shadows on the ground.

Crop mark sites are mainly caused by differences in the amount of moisture in the soil. If a Roman road is buried in a field, there will be a greater depth of topsoil (and therefore more moisture) on either side of the road than on top of it, and so crops will be stunted and will ripen earlier above the road than on either side. This

difference in the crop can be seen from the air, although unfortunately not all crops respond to differences in moisture in such a visible way. Those that do may only display the differences for a matter of weeks or even days before the whole crop ripens, so there is an element of luck in flying over the right place at the right time.

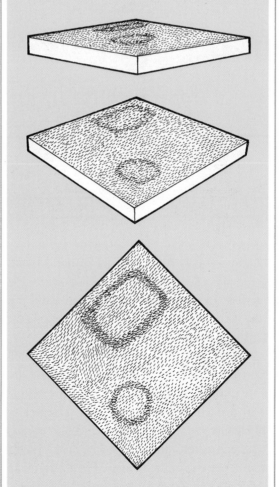

ABOVE In fields of growing crops and on parched grassland, it is possible to detect archaeological sites by cropmarks such as this small rectilinear enclosure.

LEFT The use of aerial photography in understanding cropmarks: at the top, the cropmarks seen from ground level; in the centre the cropmarks are viewed as if in an oblique aerial photograph, and below, the same cropmarks are seen as if in a vertical aerial photograph.

RIGHT Low earthworks or stone walls can be discovered from the air because of the shadows cast by them in very low sunlight.

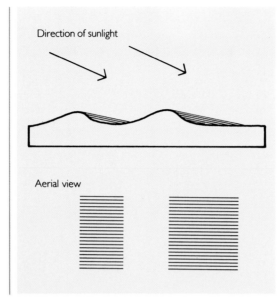

Direction of sunlight

Aerial view

BELOW Cropmarks are caused by buried features such as ditches and walls affecting the moisture content of the soil and therefore the growing rate of the crop above.

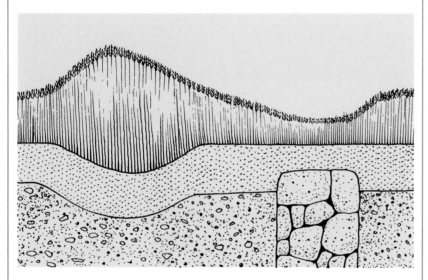

The use of infra-red photography is particularly useful in this respect. Although infra-red light is invisible to the human eye, it can be detected by special photographic film; in general, the amount of infra-red light reflected from a plant depends on its ripeness, so that infra-red photographs can produce good-contrast images of crop marks that may be hardly visible on ordinary photographic film or to the eye.

Soil mark sites are visible because of different coloured marks in the soil, usually just after ploughing. For example, if a burial mound with a ditch around it has been flattened by ploughing, the material from which the mound was constructed, the soil filling the ditch, and the soil in the rest of the ploughed field may be of different colours. This is easiest to detect when

the mound has been made of a material with a distinctive colour, such as chalk.

Shadow sites are made visible by earthworks or stone walls casting shadows in very low-level sunlight. At dawn or before sunset, or more usually in winter when the sun is low in the sky, even very low earthworks or walls cast shadows, thus betraying the presence of an archaeological site.

But while many sites can be found by using aerial photography, many cannot, such as those buried by a considerable depth of alluvium and ones hidden in woodland. Furthermore, not all patterns and marks seen on aerial photographs represent archaeological sites – crop marks and soil marks can be caused by geological features, such as fissures in the underlying rock which have filled with soil and produce patterns resembling buried sites. Patterns made in fields by the tracks of heavy machinery also frequently resemble patterns associated with archaeological remains. Consequently, great care has to be taken when interpreting marks seen on aerial photographs, and wherever possible the site should be visited on the ground to establish whether the marks have resulted from a buried archaeological site or from some other cause.

Whatever the method used to discover a new site, the most important element is to record its position and any other details that might be apparent at the time of discovery. Not only is this important in order to be able to find the site again and to make others aware of its existence, but such details may become the only record of the site. Many archaeological sites are only known from old aerial photographs taken during military operations in the 1940s and 1950s: the sites themselves have since been destroyed.

■ HOW SITES ARE LOCATED

Unless sites are discovered by accident (when a new road cuts through a prehistoric cemetery, for example) most methods of discovery do not locate sites with sufficient accuracy for excavation to take place with confidence. Aerial photographs reveal little more than the site's main features,

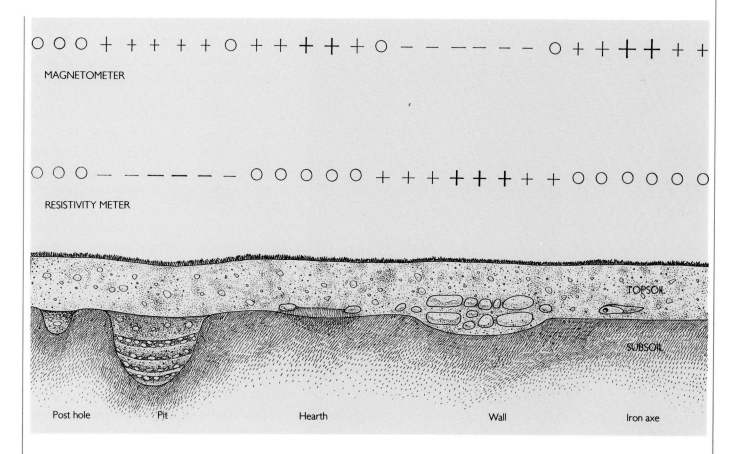

MAGNETOMETER

RESISTIVITY METER

TOPSOIL

SUBSOIL

Post hole   Pit   Hearth   Wall   Iron axe

and plotting scatters of surface finds only gives a reasonable guide to its centre, with little information about its extent or shape. Sites suspected through documentary research or for some other reason may also need to be more precisely pinpointed before excavation can take place. Various methods of locating sites have therefore been developed which attempt to give a better idea of a site's layout. The two main methods used are resistivity surveying and magnetic surveying.

Resistivity surveying is based on the principle that underground features such as masonry walls have a high resistance to an electric current, whereas filled-in features, such as ditches or pits, have a lower resistance. Used for this type of surveying are resistivity meters, operated by passing an electric current between metal probes pushed into the ground, and measuring the resistance in the ground to that current. By using a grid marked out on the ground, each point where a reading is taken can be plotted.

The results of the survey can be presented in a variety of ways, such as by 'contours', showing lines of equal readings in the same way that weather maps use contours to show lines of

equal pressure. More commonly, dot-density diagrams are used in which dots closer together (giving a darker image) portray high readings, while dots spaced further apart (giving a lighter image) portray lower readings. Nowadays, the results of nearly all such surveys are plotted by computer, which offers a wide range of diagrammatic methods to portray the results. With computer plotting, the same survey readings can be plotted in a variety of ways to extract the maximum amount of information from them. Dot-density diagrams are still the most common method of portraying results because features such as walls, which give high readings, show up as dark lines. Dot-density diagrams are therefore similar in appearance to ordinary plans and so are easier to understand.

The other main method of locating sites is by magnetic surveying. This works by detecting differences in the magnetic field of the soil using a magnetometer. These differences are caused by several factors. Solid features such as walls tend to have a smaller amount of magnetic minerals within them than the surrounding soil, and therefore give lower readings. Areas of burning,

ABOVE Various types of buried features and finds are detected in different ways by magnetic surveying (above) and by resistivity surveying (below). O is an average background reading, − a negative response, and + a positive response. The different methods do not react to the same types of buried feature, and are thus to some extent complementary.

such as hearths, give higher readings, as do filled-in features such as pits and ditches.

As with resistivity meters, readings are taken at points on a grid marked out on the ground, and the results are usually plotted in the form of computer-drawn diagrams. Many resistivity meters and magnetometers can now be fitted with a data recorder, which records the readings in computer-readable form so that the results can be fed directly into a computer as soon as the survey is finished.

Other techniques, such as echo-sounding and soil scanning radar, are currently being developed, and are likely to be used more and more in the future for accurate location and surveying of sites. Other, less scientific, methods of location are also in use. These include probing, augering and dowsing. Probing simply involves pushing a metal rod into the soil to try to determine the presence of buried features from the depth of penetration of the probe. An auger works in much the same way, but instead of being pushed into the soil, it has a corkscrew end which can be twisted down into the earth. More common are hollow augers and borers which are used to collect samples of soil and, more often, peat for environmental analysis.

Dowsing is the same procedure as water divining. The dowser uses some kind of indicator, such as a twig, metal rods, or a pendulum to

ABOVE A resistivity meter being used to survey a site.

RIGHT A trial trench being dug by hand.

show the presence or absence of archaeological features as the dowser walks over the ground. Although the mechanism by which dowsing works is not understood, the method has been shown to be capable of accurately locating buried archaeological features.

With all three methods outlined above, the best results are obtained by conducting a systematic survey, usually on a marked-out grid, so that the results can be plotted as a plan of the site.

None of the current methods of locating sites is totally accurate, however. The most common fault is that important features are not always revealed by these methods, which can lead to the excavation being sited wrongly. As the only certain way to locate buried features is to excavate them, trial trenches are often dug to confirm the results of a survey before the main

excavation takes place. Sometimes trial trenching is the primary method used for location, either because the resources for a resistivity or magnetic survey are not available, or because they would be inappropriate. The problem with trial trenches is that if they are very small it is easy to miss the main features of a site, yet the larger the trenches used, the nearer the process becomes to full-scale excavation. Trenches can be dug by machine, although it is difficult to recognize archaeological features as a machine is uncovering, and perhaps cutting through them. For this reason, machine-cut trial trenches are most commonly used on sites where there is insufficient time for more careful methods. Whenever possible, trial trenches are dug by hand, because these always provide more information than machine-dug trenches of the same size.

ABOVE Here a trial trench has established the presence of early Christian graves in Bangor, Wales. Such trial trenches are far more cost-effective than undertaking a full-scale excavation without being sure if archaeological features survive on a site.

ABOVE The site at Ebla, north Syria, being excavated by a series of small trenches, a system pioneered by Sir Mortimer Wheeler but not now commonly used.

One way of looking at a site is to examine its stratigraphy – the sequence of layers that have been laid down one on top of another to form the site itself. This is done by leaving vertical faces (called sections) as the excavation proceeds, so that the layers visible in those sections can be recorded and studied. Another way of looking at a site is to concentrate on its plan, and to see how this changes with time. For example, there may be evidence for a sequence of buildings being constructed and going out of use over a long period of time. To study this changing pattern, large areas of the site are usually excavated simultaneously so that the plans of buildings and other structures can be better understood.

Ideally, an archaeologist wants to obtain as

EXCAVATION

Excavation, the unearthing, examination, and recording of archaeological sites, is most people's idea of archaeology, despite the fact that in many countries far more valuable work is done by accurately locating and plotting unknown sites, rather than by excavation. Very time-consuming, labour intensive and an expensive part of arch-aeology, the very processes of excavation also destroys the site: complete excavation is complete destruction, and so excavation is often described as an 'unrepeatable experiment'. No two sites are exactly alike, and so the excavation of a site such as a burial mound cannot be duplicated by excavating another burial mound. For this reason, archaeologists bear a heavy responsibility to make comprehensive records of everything that they find and observe, because no one else will ever have another chance to do so.

Excavation is best thought of as a post-mortem examination of an archaeological site, and involves a detailed dissection of a site in order to gain as much information as possible.

There are three kinds of excavation: re-search, rescue and salvage. Research excavations are conducted primarily to test hypotheses and to answer questions that have arisen out of arch-aeological research. Rescue excavations are those conducted on sites that are threatened with de-struction and should be carried out to at least the same standards as found on research excavations. Salvage excavations are those carried out on sites where destruction has already begun, often be-cause the site was unknown before construction work started. In this situation, it is very difficult to maintain high standards, as such work usually has to be done within a short time limit, and often with very little space. Under such condi-tions, any information about the site that can be salvaged is regarded as a bonus. Unfortunately, in some situations there is insufficient time to complete a rescue excavation and the work may have to be continued as a salvage operation.

RIGHT A derelict medieval barn prior to conversion to housing units. When sites such as this are to be destroyed, it is important that the building above the ground is recorded before it is destroyed, as well as the ground beneath being excavated.

BELOW Recording the changing plan of a site is one of the key tasks during an excavation.

ABOVE An exca
Bronze Age te
Assad in north
of medium-siz
being used.

open area leaves very few, if any, sections that show the complete stratigraphy of the site. One solution to this problem, used by Mortimer Wheeler, is to excavate a site in a series of medium-sized trenches laid out on a grid system. The trench sides provide information about the stratigraphy, and can eventually be removed to give an unobstructed view of the plan. At the opposite end of the spectrum, another solution is to excavate one large area without sections, but to build up a picture of the stratigraphy by recording the relationship of each layer to any adjoining layers. In practice, since each site is unique, archaeologists use the mixture of large-scale area excavation and sections that seems most appropriate to the site.

On most excavations, the first operation is to remove the modern deposits covering the archaeological levels. This overburden may be only a shallow layer of topsoil or a deep layer of modern building rubble, as is the case on some urban sites, and it may be removed by digging with hand tools or by using a mechanical excavator, depending on the site.

Once it is suspected that the archaeological levels have been reached or almost reached, the excavation area is cleaned up using hand tools, and all the loose earth is removed so that any differences in the colour and texture of the soil can be distinguished. On sites where there are no walls or other solid remains, those differences alone show the presence of archaeological fea-

BELOW A rescue site being excavated as an area excavation, with stretches of ditches excavated leaving vertical sections to provide more information.

much information as possible about both the stratigraphy of a site and its plan, but there is a conflict between the two approaches. If, for example, the site is excavated in a series of small trenches in order to gain the maximum amount of information about the stratigraphy, it is then very difficult to understand the plan view of the site. On the other hand, excavation of a large

tures, such as pits and ditches that have silted up or have been filled in. Once such differences in the soil can be detected, the archaeological features are excavated, often by first removing what appears to be the latest (uppermost) layer, and then proceeding to the next layer, and so on.

The way the digging is done depends on the nature of the site. All kinds of hand tools, ranging from picks, mattocks and shovels down to builders' pointing trowels and even teaspoons and paintbrushes, are used. Samples of the soil, and in some cases all the excavated soil, may be kept for dry sieving or wet sieving in order to retrieve environmental evidence and very small finds. The exact manner in which the excavation proceeds can vary considerably depending on the site's characteristics, and there are usually several possible strategies that can be followed in any particular situation. For every site, however, the archaeologists' main concerns are to recover the sequence of plans that result from the changing occupation and use of the site over a period of time; the stratigraphic sequence of layers; the relationship of any features such as walls, pits and ditches to one another; evidence for the dating of these features and of the site as a whole; evidence for the climate and local environment when the site was occupied; and the relationship of the site to other sites, both in the locality and further afield. With all of these factors in mind, the archaeologists work out the excavation strategy as the excavation proceeds, to build as complete a picture of the site as possible.

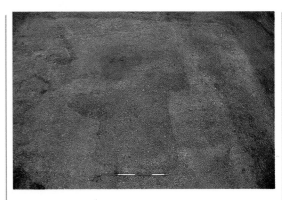

Apart from physically digging a site, recording the evidence is of particular importance. While the sequence of excavation cannot be decided until the nature of the site becomes apparent, the methods of recording the information are determined in advance. There are three main types of record that are made: drawn records, photographic records, and written records.

Drawn records consist of detailed plans, often at a scale of 1:20 or 1:10, section drawings, usually at a scale of 1:10, and any other drawings (such as detailed drawings of skeletons), that may be considered necessary. Plans may be drawn showing only the outlines of layers and features such as walls and pits, or they may be drawn showing everything that is visible, including all stones larger than ½ in (1 cm) in diameter. Drawings of sections usually portray everything that can be seen, including the boundaries between layers, because this information may provide clues to the processes by which the layers have been deposited. The amount of detail and the scale of the drawings vary according to the type of site and the time and resources available.

The photographic record of an excavation usually comprises detailed photographs of specific parts of the site and of the site as a whole. The photographs are most commonly taken using two cameras, one with a black and white print film and the other with a colour transparency film. This duplication is necessary because some differences in the colour and texture of soil are easier to see on black and white photographs and some are easier to see in colour. One photographic technique, called photogrammetry, is sometimes used to supplement or even replace plans by taking vertical photographs of the site from a constant height, in much the same way as

BELOW Clearing the modern deposits from an archaeological site is often done using a machine, with an archaeologist keeping watch in case anything is uncovered by the machine.

LEFT A large feature is revealed as a dark stain in the gravel.

RIGHT On excavation, the same feature is shown to be an impressive Iron Age grave; the body had been buried with a chariot.

ABOVE Many different types of tools and digging techniques are used to excavate sites. Here an area excavation is being used to examine a shallow rural site.

RIGHT Some unusual tools can be employed, such as this vacuum cleaner which is helping to expose the remains of a human burial at Sutton Hoo, Suffolk, England.

maps are produced using aerial photography. In a few excavations, video cameras are also used. These are useful not only for recording what is being excavated, but also to show the methods of excavation that are used.

Written excavation records once consisted of observations written down in a notebook, but nowadays most archaeologists use printed forms, or even a series of forms, which are filled in to record the evidence not covered by the drawn and photographic records. The use of forms helps to standardize the recording procedures, and also serves as a reminder of what observations to make and what to look for. Recorded in this way, the information is easier to sort and analyse after the excavation has finished. Some excavators use a tape recorder, and the recordings are later transcribed, but this type of recording tends to be in addition to, rather than in place of, the more structured recording on printed forms. Experiments using portable computers at excavation sites, in order to enter the written record on to computer at that stage, have been tried. But normally the information on the recording forms is checked and corrected first and then entered on to computer after the excavation has been completed.

It is a vital part of the written records that the exact place where every find was discovered is noted, particularly important because finds can yield a great deal of information. For example, it is essential to know exactly where each find was unearthed in order to assess whether the date of the finds can help to date the deposits in which they were found. Recording the exact findspot of every find can also reveal what activities took place in particular parts of the site – for example, a concentration of slag and crucibles may indicate that an area was used for metalworking.

When the excavation is over, all that is left is the records that the archaeologists have compiled. Archaeologists have a clear responsibility: until the information contained in those records is made available to other archaeologists, and to the general public, the excavation is not complete: the information is still as inaccessible as if the site had never been excavated, and the records themselves might just as well be buried.

■ PROBLEMS AND LIMITATIONS OF EXCAVATION

One of the main problems of archaeological excavation is coping with the weather. Apart from the discomfort of rain, cold, wind or excessive heat, the amount of moisture in the soil affects the visibility of the layers that are being excavated. If the soil is too wet, only the most obvious features are likely to be clearly visible, while if the soil is too dry, no differences in soil colour and texture may be distinguishable at all. So in almost any weather conditions, there is a great

BELOW The type of tools and techniques used in excavation varies with the country and climate, and the resources available. This excavation is taking place at Tel Halawa, a 3rd millenium tell on the Euphrates, which has remains of stone and mud brick buildings.

danger of not being able to see and record soil layers properly.

In countries where too much moisture is more likely than too little, such as in northern Europe, steps are often taken to have portable shelters or covers available to keep parts of the site dry, and in some cases temporary structures are built to cover the whole site for the duration of the excavation. This is also done on some long-running excavations of exceptionally important sites to enable excavation to continue all the year round under controlled conditions.

In areas where the site is likely to be too dry, there is often more of a problem, since water for moistening the site is generally scarce in such areas. As a general rule, though, it is easier to cope with a dry site than a wet one: as long as a water supply is available, a dry site can be moistened to highlight the differences in soil colour and texture.

Apart from these, there are also underwater sites, and land sites which are actually waterlogged. These rarely have anything approaching the variety of colour of soil that normally occurs on dry land sites, and excavators have to rely much more on the different textures in the material being excavated. It is possible to protect the excavators from inclement weather conditions, such as by the use of shelters, but the sites themselves cannot be dried out as the waterlogging actually preserves the sites.

Another major limiting factor in excavation is the subjective nature of the excavation process. As each excavator removes a layer of soil, decisions have to be constantly made: whether that soil is part of the layer which has just been removed or part of another layer; where the boundaries to that layer are; what the relationship of the layer is to the adjoining layers; whether a soil sample is required; and so on. This situation applies to everyone actually digging on a site, so as there may be anything between one and 100 people all constantly taking decisions in this way, there exists a large potential for error. Such errors show up from time to time as inconsistencies in the records, but much worse are those that go undetected, and which could lead to the wrong conclusions being drawn when the records are analysed.

On many excavations this potential for error is reduced as far as possible by putting the workforce under the control of supervisors, who are in turn responsible to one or more directors. The director of an excavation determines the overall strategy and provides advice to the supervisors, while the supervisors provide guidance and advice to the workforce. With this sort of hierarchical team, the possibility of idiosyncratic judgements is minimized, and with the control of the recording in the supervisors' hands, errors are more readily noted at the time they occur and can be corrected or allowed for in the subsequent analysis. No system is perfect, though, and a great deal still depends on the skill and

BELOW Making a detailed scale drawing of a vertical section can take as long as excavating the feature in the first place.

BELOW BOTTOM Photographic recording of an excavation is improved if a scaffolding tower is available for aerial views of the site.

RIGHT Aerial views of an excavation can also be obtained by suspending a camera from a kite.

experience of the excavation team; to a larger extent, an excavation is only as good as its excavators.

POST-EXCAVATION ANALYSIS

Once an excavation finishes, the archaeologist is left with numerous written, drawn and photographic records in addition to a quantity of finds and environmental samples with which to establish a picture of the history and development of the excavated site. Post-excavation analysis turns these raw records into meaningful information. Carried out behind closed doors – in workrooms, laboratories and offices – it rarely gets a mention in the media despite the fact that excavations are often featured. In fact, depending on the size of the excavation and the range of finds, more people may be engaged in the post-excavation analysis than during the actual excavation; and whatever the size of the site, the post-excavation analysis takes at least twice as long as the excavation itself.

Before any finds are washed and marked, they have to be sorted to see which are in need of conservation. The most usual category of finds needing conservation is metalwork, but this can often remain in a stable condition for several months; on the other hand, finds such as those of wood or leather require immediate conservation on site as they are excavated. Finds that are

ABOVE Photography of details of many parts of the site (in colour or black and white) is an essential part of the excavation recording process.

RIGHT The use of Electronic Distance Measurement (EDM) is a very accurate method of undertaking surveys and of establishing the precise location of finds on an excavation.

LEFT The recording and checking of written notes and scale drawings is an essential and time-consuming part of an excavation.

BELOW The use of portable computers on an excavation may eventually replace the use of record sheets.

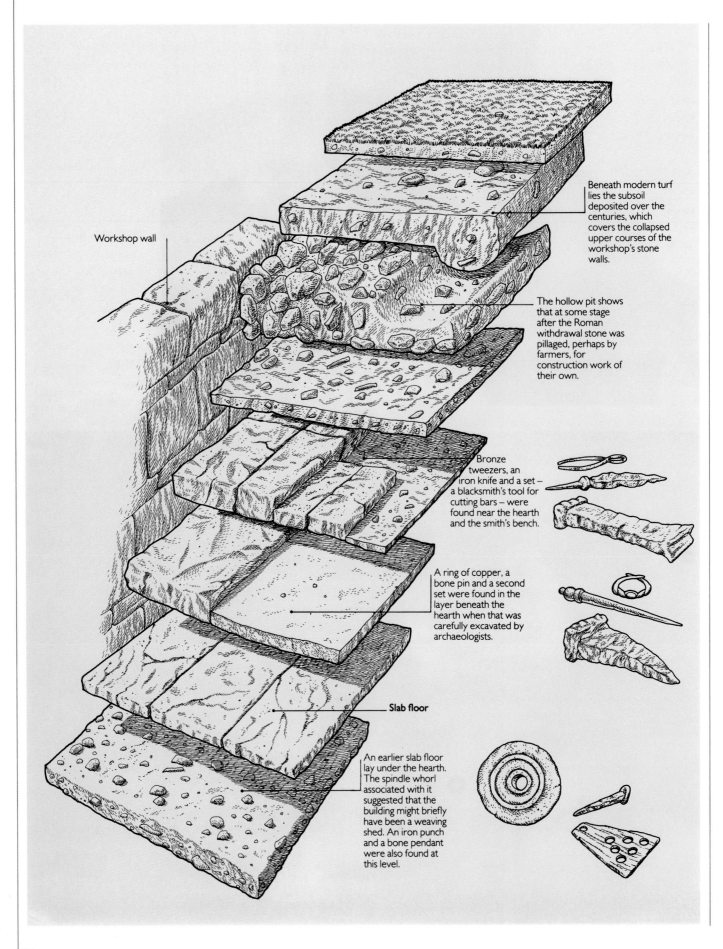

Workshop wall

Beneath modern turf lies the subsoil deposited over the centuries, which covers the collapsed upper courses of the workshop's stone walls.

The hollow pit shows that at some stage after the Roman withdrawal stone was pillaged, perhaps by farmers, for construction work of their own.

Bronze tweezers, an iron knife and a set – a blacksmith's tool for cutting bars – were found near the hearth and the smith's bench.

A ring of copper, a bone pin and a second set were found in the layer beneath the hearth when that was carefully excavated by archaeologists.

Slab floor

An earlier slab floor lay under the hearth. The spindle whorl associated with it suggested that the building might briefly have been a weaving shed. An iron punch and a bone pendant were also found at this level.

LEFT The exact recording of layers and their finds can give many clues to the history of a site. This is a reconstruction of the vertical excavation of a 4th-century Roman workshop near Bristol, England.

RIGHT The weather can greatly affect the progress of work on a site. Rescue excavation is here taking place despite the very wet conditions.

BELOW In countries where rain is likely to be a problem, shelters can be erected under which excavation can take place in all weathers.

RIGHT On very dry sites, water can be used to bring out different soil colours. Here a vertical section is being sprayed with water prior to recording by photography and drawing.

BELOW In both dry and wet countries, large purpose-built shelters erected over the excavation are an invaluable means of allowing the excavation to continue all-year-round, and to allow visitors to view the excavation. Such shelters are rarely used, though, because of their expense.

fragile or should not be washed for any other reason (such as metalwork) are also sorted at this stage.

While the excavation was in progress, it may have been possible to wash some of the finds and mark each one with a code indicating where it was found: this task has to be completed before any further work can be done. The quantity of finds depends on the type of site being excavated, and for sites that produce a large quantity of finds, the tasks of washing and marking them can be lengthy. An excavation of a Roman villa, for example, can produce several tons of small fragments of pottery, glass and tiles.

The washed and marked finds are then sorted into groups such as sherds of coarse pottery, sherds of glazed pottery, all the prehistoric worked flint, and so on, and are studied by specialists who prepare reports on them.

Once this is done, the archaeologists start to deal with the records of the excavation. Apart from the finds, these represent all that is left of the excavated site, and so are extremely important; they also represent the investment in the excavation from a financial point of view, which may have cost a considerable amount of money, and it is therefore usual to duplicate them, storing one copy far away from the original records in case of accidents. This is easy enough with record sheets and drawings, which can simply be photocopied or put on to microfilm, but is far more of a problem with a photographic record comprising hundreds or thousands of slides and photographs. Usually, the black and white photographic negatives are stored in one place, and the black and white prints and the colour slides are stored elsewhere, all ideally in fireproof safes.

The first stage in analysing the records is to scrutinize each individual record to ensure that it is in order, fully complete, and that any noticeable errors are corrected where possible. The detailed catalogue of photographs should be

BELOW Whatever the conditions of the excavation, high standards of recording and excavation should always be maintained. In the foreground part of an oven is being excavated, while behind a draughtsperson is doing a scale plan of part of the site.

cross-referenced to the written records at this stage, so that the photographs can be used to the full in the post-excavation analysis.

The next task is to establish the relationships between all the layers on the site. Each layer or part of a layer is usually called a 'context', and each is given a unique identifying number during the excavation. Separate records are made for each context, and any finds are given the same unique number. On most sites, the relationship between contexts is drawn as a matrix diagram, which is rather like a family tree. Using this diagram, it is possible to see at a glance the relationship of one context to the rest of the site. Compiling such a matrix diagram requires a detailed study of all the records, however, and inevitably there will be some gaps in the diagram where it was not possible to establish the precise relationship between some contexts during the excavation itself.

The matrix diagram also provides a basic framework for working out the phases of the site. For example, it may be possible to determine that one group of contexts represents a building,

BELOW Waterlogged sites are much more difficult to excavate, but the amount of material that survives can be remarkable. These represent some of the thousands of fragments of wood from Flag Fen, England.

RIGHT It is essential that excavated finds are washed clean and their context number marked on them with waterproof ink.

which was covered by a group of contexts representing a paved area, which in turn was covered by a group of contexts representing another building, etc. A sequence of events – or phases – can be established: a phase when the first building was in use, a phase when the paved area was in use, and a phase when the second building was in use. What is more difficult to establish is whether the first building was inhabited for a while, demolished just after the inhabitants moved out, immediately paved over, and a new building later constructed; or whether the first building was inhabited for a while, abandoned by its inhabitants for many years, then collapsed through decay, was paved over later on, and then a second building constructed. If the records are studied sufficiently well, such evidence may become apparent, and the first glimpses of the site's history begin to emerge.

Once this has been done, the information on each phase of the site can be amalgamated with the information from the specialist reports on the finds (if these have been finished) and with any information from other sources, such as radiocarbon dates. The specialist reports usually include information about the dating of finds and other significant points, such as evidence for trade or contact with other contemporary sites. Archaeologists have to judge the importance of the information in each case, and how it relates to the analysis. For example, if pottery from a pit is said to be of a particular date by the specialist, a decision has to be taken as to how, if at all, that date relates to the pit in which the pottery was found. It may, in fact, date the pit very accurately.

Once all the information has been incorporated, the sequence of phases will have been assigned dates at various points, although these will be of differing quality: some may be accurate to a few years, others only to the nearest couple of centuries. Nevertheless, the skeleton structure formed by the relationship between the contexts, dated wherever possible by finds or by scientific methods, gives the outline of the history of the site as far as it can be known.

All this data is then written up as a technical report, and forms part of the information stored as an archive for future reference. This detailed archive report attempts to explain what each group of contexts represents – buildings, structures, rubbish deposits, and so on – and is used as the basis for writing a more concise report for publication.

This published report aims to provide a basic summary of the information about the excavated site for use by other archaeologists. The amount of detail included in such a report varies considerably, but it is always a much condensed version of the information contained in the archive, which would be far too costly to publish in its entirety. When preparing it, the archaeologist not only has to consider the text, but also what illustrations to include. Maps and plans showing site information are nearly always included, but the number and type of photographs and of illustrations of other details of the site and of finds vary from site to site. Anybody who needs to study a site in detail should look at the archive as well as the published report.

Once the report is ready for publication, the archaeologist may then write a book or book-let on the excavation in terms that the general reader can understand. A great deal of jargon and many technical terms are used by archaeologists, and they can make excavation reports fairly incomprehensible. (Such jargon does contribute, however, as archaeology deals with many sites, objects, and even tribes and nations whose actual names are unknown.) Without a more general explanation, the information gained from the excavation may take a while to reach the general public. Otherwise information is filtered through other books: for example, an archaeologist studying the archaeology of a particular region might publish a book which includes a summary of the site information, and which in turn is used as a source by someone writing a school textbook. Years after the excavation took place, it may come to the notice of schoolchildren studying history, but by this time, the site that required so much work to gain so much information is likely to be described in just one or two sentences.

FAR RIGHT Bulky finds such as fragments of Roman painted plaster can be found in huge quantities on excavations, and therefore pose a particular problem during post-excavation work; much space is needed to sort, reconstruct and record them.

BELOW A small area of painted Roman plaster that has been reconstructed.

YESTERDAY'S RUBBISH

ABOVE Washed finds including
fragments of leather awaiting
conservation and the residue
from wet sieving.

WHAT ARE FINDS?

Although finds can be spectacular objects like the gold mask on Tutankhamun's mummy, or the pair of gold and millefiori glass shoulder clasps from Sutton Hoo, to an archaeologist, the term covers anything portable that can provide information about an archaeological site. The dividing line between a fixed 'site' and a portable 'find' is often a narrow one: for example, the site of the ship *Mary Rose* was excavated over a period of several years, but when the remains of the ship itself were eventually raised, they were treated like any other waterlogged find, albeit on a much larger scale. The same is true of standing monuments such as tombstones – it is difficult to know whether to categorize these as sites or finds.

The majority of finds consist of objects, or more frequently fragments of objects, that have been lost, thrown away or deliberately buried. These are not necessarily human-made objects, since finds include anything like animal bones and insect remains. Deliberately buried either as ritual offerings to accompany the burial of the dead, as gifts to the gods, or else to keep objects safe, finds can also be buried as a means of disposal. Rubbish from a household was often buried in pits, and would have included worn out and broken objects in addition to food debris such as animal bones and oyster shells.

BELOW It is difficult to categorize some rock paintings and carvings as they can be regarded as sites or finds. But where they are subject to decay or vandalism, they are sometimes set up as finds for display in museums. This is an Indian petroglyph in Albuquerque, USA, in its original position.

Most finds that were simply lost (small and easily mislaid, such as coins and brooches) or objects that fell into places from which they could not be retrieved, such as wells, are often complete and may be in very good condition, depending on the materials from which they are made and the conditions in which they have been buried. By contrast, most objects thrown away

were by definition worn out, broken, or regarded as useless. Discarded fragments of objects are the most common type of find on archaeological sites, and consequently it is this 'yesterday's rubbish' that provides most information about the site and the people who used it.

Excavation finds are given an identifying code number to record the layer in which they were discovered. For finds of special significance (sometimes called 'small finds'), the exact find-spot is also measured and recorded. On sites where they are scarce, each is recorded like a small find, although on many sites the sheer quantity of finds makes this impossible.

Most finds are sufficiently robust to be washed in clean cold water with brushes (such

ABOVE Tombstones and other carved monuments such as these remains of early Christian crosses can also be treated as finds even if they are still in their original positions.

ABOVE A waterlogged wooden ladder being excavated.

ABOVE RIGHT The same ladder after excavation and conservation.

as toothbrushes) and they are then left to dry. But finds that are deteriorating (such as iron objects which corrode rapidly in damp conditions), that have been preserved by unusual conditions (such as waterlogged wood or leather which dry out and warp or crumble if left untreated), or any others which are fragile may need conservation in a laboratory to prevent further decay and to strengthen them, so that they can be handled and studied.

Fragments of building debris can form a large part of the total number of finds from a site. For example, the excavation on a Roman town house will yield pieces of roof tiles, floor tiles, fragments of mosaic floors, broken window glass, and so on. All these can provide information about the site, giving clues as to what the roof looked like, where the floor tiles were made, and how many of the floors had mosaics.

Environmental evidence forms a special category of finds, and can consist of animal bones and snail shells large enough to be seen and collected by the excavators. It may also include very small remains such as pollen grains, that can only be seen and identified with the aid of a microscope. Because in most cases environmental specialists need to undertake statistical analysis of the information, samples are normally taken as part of a systematic programme of environmental sampling. Soil can be taken to recover pollen grains, tiny snail shells, seeds, small fish and bird bones and insect remains, all of which can provide evidence about the immediate environment of the site when it was occupied. Wet-sieving, or flotation, is used to recover these organic remains from the soil by turning soil samples into a very wet mud. Heavy unwanted particles sink, and lighter particles, such as tiny plant and animal remains, float off and are collected in a sieve.

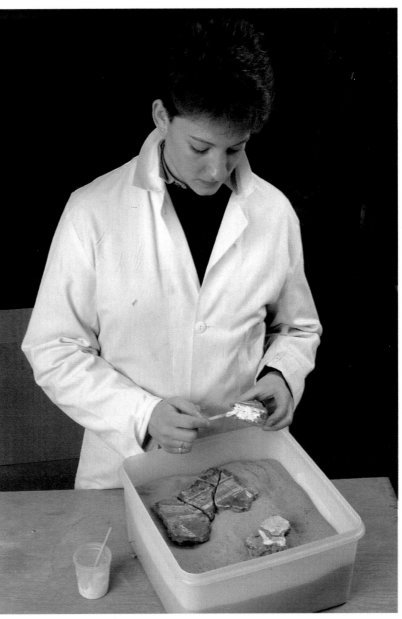

Finds which are not recovered during excavation, but are discovered by accident or are found on the surface of the ground during a field survey, are sometimes called stray finds. Their main significance is an indication of a possible archaeological site near to where they were recovered. For this reason, it is most important to know exactly where each find was discovered. By plotting the position of stray finds on a map, it is often possible to pinpoint the archaeological site from which they came. If a site is being destroyed slowly, only a few finds are brought to the surface at any one time, and it may take years of plotting before the whereabouts of the site becomes apparent. So no matter how insignificant at the time, it is important that all finds are reported and properly recorded.

Many aspects of the site, including dating, are revealed by its finds, and it is often necessary to compare finds with those discovered elsewhere. It is often the most common and mundane finds, such as sherds of broken pottery, that prove the most useful: a spectacular find usually provides relatively little information because it is so rare.

■ TECHNIQUES OF FINDS ANALYSIS

Once finds from an excavation have been washed and marked with identifying codes, the initial part of the finds analysis is usually done by the director of the excavation. First of all they are sorted into groups of similar material: pottery, brooches, pieces of worked stone, and so on; these may be sent at this stage to various specialists, who will study them and write a technical report. Nowadays, however, specialists often restrict themselves not only to a particular type of find, but also to a specific archaeological period.

ABOVE LEFT Marking finds with an identifying code using a mapping pen and waterproof ink.

ABOVE A conservator reconstructing pieces of painted plaster.

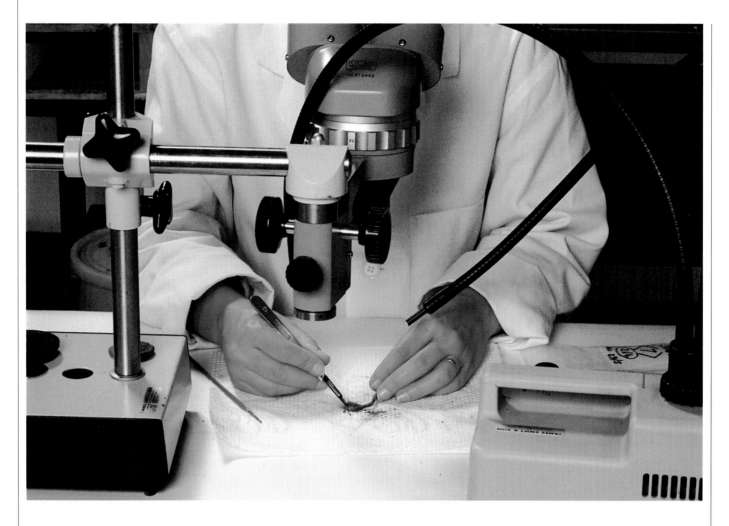

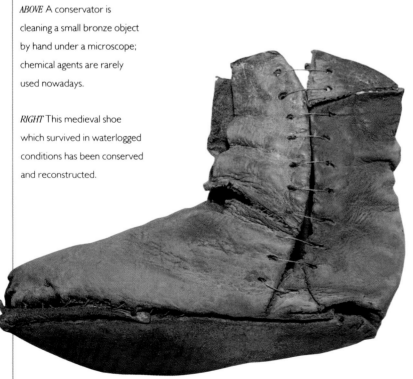

ABOVE A conservator is cleaning a small bronze object by hand under a microscope; chemical agents are rarely used nowadays.

RIGHT This medieval shoe which survived in waterlogged conditions has been conserved and reconstructed.

As a result, these finds often need to be sorted into further groups such as pre-Inca pottery and Inca pottery before they are studied.

For some types of find, scientific methods are useful in the process of analysis, but most specialists begin their analysis in the same basic way. The finds are laid out on work surfaces and are sorted into groups of similar material, either in a single stage if there are very few, or in batches. With sherds of pottery, groups will be made initially according to the colour of the pottery and any other indicators such as the way the surface of the pottery is finished, any distinctive inclusions in the clay such as quartz, and so on. These are then sub-divided by sorting the sherds in each group into rim sherds (from the top of the pot), base sherds (from the bottom of the pot), fragments of handles, and body sherds (sherds from any other part of the pot that cannot be recognized as the base, rim or handle).

All this examination of the pottery is done purely by eye, sometimes with the assistance of a

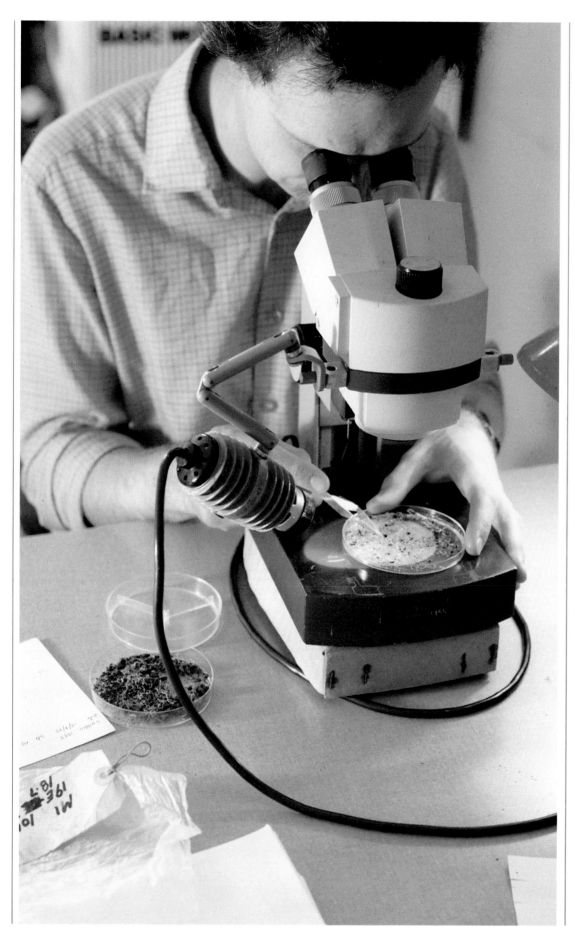

LEFT Tiny plant and animal remains, retrieved through wet sieving, are sorted and studied under a microscope.

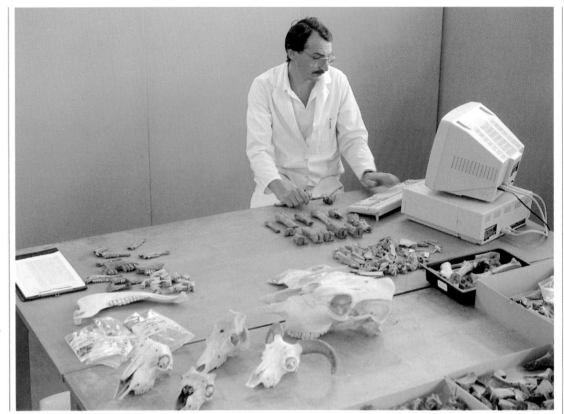

RIGHT A bone specialist is sorting animal bones into groups and entering the data on to a computer for analysis.

BELOW Numerous quantities of animal bones are found on some excavations, and each piece has to be identified, measured and recorded.

hand lens or a microscope, and is a process of subjective judgement. While there are some objective scientific analyses that can be used at this point, depending on the type of pottery being studied, for pottery from most excavations the analysis depends on the specialist's judgement.

Next is the detailed examination and cataloguing of each sherd of pottery. A record is made of details such as where on the site a sherd was found, its colour, type of fabric, and decoration. Sometimes a sketch drawing of the sherd is done to show significant features. Quite often at this stage, sherds will be selected for illustration in the published report, and any joins between sherds will be looked for. Looking for sherds

that will join together is a very time-consuming process, and is only usually done thoroughly if it is suspected that such joins exist and will add significantly to the evidence.

Specialists identify and ascribe a date to the pottery by comparison with other pottery of known date, in much the same way as antique dealers look at the features and form of an object in order to date it. As far as possible, a specialist will compare the pottery with other examples (usually called 'parallels') that have been securely dated, but if the only other examples of a type of pottery are not so well dated, the specialist points this out, giving references to the parallels that have been used.

ABOVE LEFT This drawing of an anthropomorphic glazed medieval jug from London was produced for publication.

ABOVE Wet sieving for small plant and animal remains can be done using simple equipment; on this excavation, sieves, a hosepipe and a dustbin are being used.

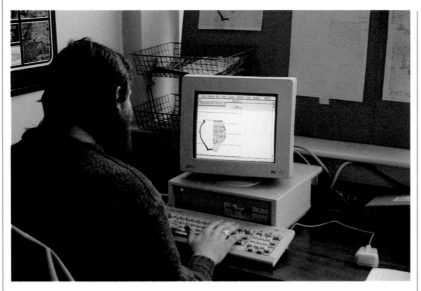

ABOVE Computers are invaluable in many forms of finds analysis. A computer is being used here to record types of pottery. When all the data is entered on to the computer, it can then be sorted in numerous ways which would be too time-consuming using manual methods.

Once the catalogue is written, the specialist calculates the quantities of each type of pottery that have come from each layer and makes observations about the significance of the groups of pottery. If the data has been put on computer, this quantification is easier. All this detailed analysis and cataloguing of the pottery forms part of the archive for the excavation, and the specialist then produces a much shorter report for publication, giving the main results of the analysis. Some specialists will both advise on which sherds are to be drawn and will do the drawings required, but otherwise the selected sherds are sent to an archaeological illustrator while the reports for archive and for publication are returned to the excavator.

Although this example has dealt with the analysis of pottery, the same basic approach of identification, sorting, grouping, quantification, comparison with examples from elsewhere, and the formulation of conclusions from the evidence is used in the study of most finds and environmental samples. The main differences between specialists studying different types of finds is in the scientific methods of analysis available.

Various kinds of basic chemical analysis can be used on ceramic objects such as pottery, brick and tile, and on metal objects. Chemical analysis is usually employed to determine the materials from which an object is made, and often to identify trace elements which may give a clue to the origins and date of the object. With some pottery, chemical analysis can also be used to discover what the pottery vessel may have once contained or have been used for.

Petrological examination can be used on ceramic artefacts and on stone objects. By determining the composition of the object, it can be compared with natural sources of clay (in the case of ceramics) or stone and can indicate where the object originally came from. This method of examination involves cutting a very thin slice from the object, which is fixed to a microscope slide and ground down until it is only 0.02mm thick. This can then be studied under a microscope, and the minerals present can be identified.

Various types of spectrometry, such as optical emission spectrometry, infra-red absorption spectrometry, and atomic absorption spectrometry, can also be used to identify the constituent components of an object. Such analyses use various methods to induce a sample from the object to produce a spectrum of light. The resulting spectrum is characteristic of the elements present in the sample, and the percentage of each element can be calculated.

For objects of metal that cannot be identified, such as very misshapen corroded iron, radiography can be used. An X-ray camera, similar to ones used in hospitals, provides a picture of the solid metal and other materials that survive beneath the corrosion, and gives an idea of the original shape of the object. This is particularly useful for objects made of several different materials, such as an iron dagger with a handle inlaid with bone and enamels, since the iron corrosion often obscures such details.

Environmental evidence is often regarded as a special case, but in fact many of the standard techniques of finds analysis are also applied to the study of environmental samples. Take, for example, animal bones. Identified and sorted into groups representing the types and parts of animals from which they come, a catalogue of the bones is compiled including bone measurement which indicates the size of the animals and even their age at death. Signs of butchering, indicating that the animals were used for food, evidence of diseases, and other distinguishing features are also noted and quantified.

Pollen analysis (palynology) is mainly used to give an idea of the vegetation around an arch-

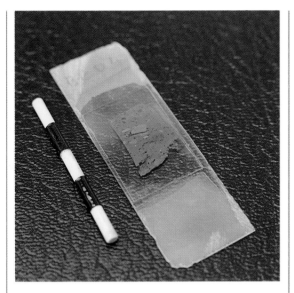

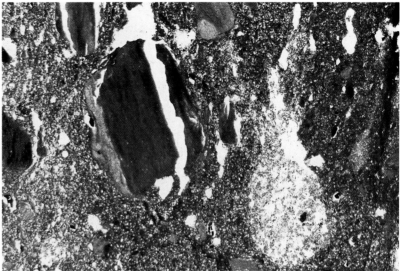

aeological site. It can provide evidence of the history and development of vegetation in a region. Pollen grains from a sample are identified and counted under a microscope, and the resulting percentages of pollens from various plants, shrubs and trees are normally presented in diagrammatic form, which allows the mixture of vegetation at any one time to be understood and compared with that of other sites.

Obviously, pollen grains are very small plant remains, and cannot be seen without the aid of a microscope; but larger remains (macroscopic plant remains), such as seeds and grains, leaves, twigs, wood and charcoal also provide evidence about the vegetation that existed around a site, and can show if and how it was exploited by the people living there. Similarly, insects and land snail shells are identified, sorted and quantified in the same way as animal and plant remains. Shells from marine and freshwater molluscs often provide evidence of the food eaten by inhabitants. The study of microscopic parasites and even

ABOVE LEFT Petrological analysis involves the use of thin sections. A thin slice (section) of a clay or stone object is mounted on a microscope slide such as this.

ABOVE Under a microscope, the constituents of the clay or stone can be identified, and the original source of the material pinpointed.

LEFT Iron objects are best drawn with the aid of X-rays which can give the shape and form of an object under the corrosion.

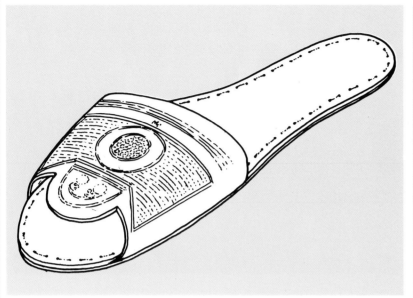

■ WHAT FINDS CAN TELL US

One of the most important aspects of archaeology, in which finds play a key role, is the dating of archaeological sites. The role of finds in dating is looked at in the next chapter, but perhaps the most obvious way in which finds can tell us about the past is by providing evidence about ancient technology. It is possible, by examination and experiment, to work out the process of manufacture in many cases, and as much of the technology used in the past is still in use today, this boils down to testing hypotheses (rather than guesswork). For example, by looking at a pot, it may be suspected that it has not been thrown on a wheel but has been made from coils of clay, joined together and smoothed by hand to form the wall of the pot. This can be tested both by examining the structure of the pot itself and by making a similar pot in this way to see if the result matches the pot being studied. Similarly, metallurgical examination of an iron tool can suggest its method of manufacture, the temperatures used, and the conditions needed in the furnace when the metal was being smelted and when it was being forged. This information can then be used to

ABOVE The careful conservation, analysis and drawing of archaeological finds can yield a good deal of information. A Roman shoe has been reconstructed by drawing and studying the surviving piece of leather (right), often using a microscope, which showed that the leather had finely stamped and tooled patterns and was also gilded.

FAR RIGHT A hand-made Bronze Age urn, originally used to contain a human cremation, after conservation and restoration.

bacteria (that can survive in exceptional conditions) gives an indication of the health and living conditions on the site, and of the diseases suffered by people living there.

The initial, almost routine, analysis of all types of finds from an excavation is only the start of the process of extracting information from the raw data that the finds provide. By studying similar finds from different sites, a great deal more information can be recovered from such things as broken pottery or rusty iron.

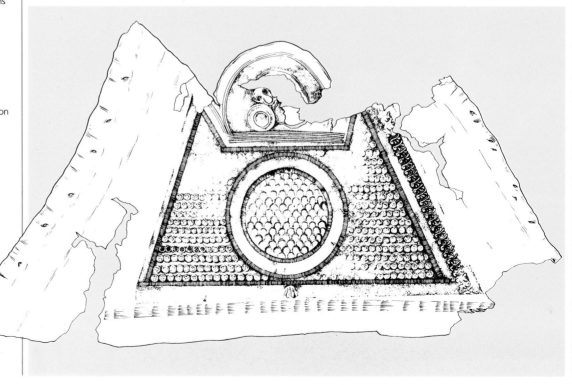

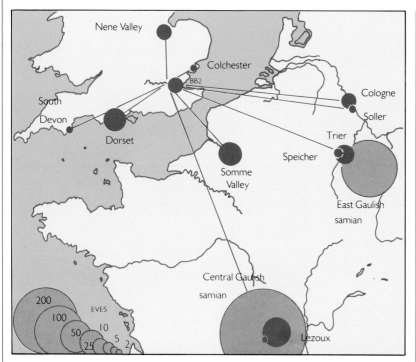

ABOVE The analysis of finds can indicate the export and trade of goods. The sources of pottery found on a Roman site in London in the 3rd century can be seen to be widespread. 'EVES' (estimated vessel equivalent method) is a means of quantifying the original numbers of pots represented.

test experimental reconstructions of furnaces found in excavations in order to establish whether or not the metal could have been smelted in a particular type of furnace, or forged at a particular type of hearth. By carefully assembling the pieces of evidence in this way, a picture of the technology in use at any one time can be built up.

The movement of artefacts between one place and another is often loosely called 'trade', a term which some archaeologists object to as the mechanism by which finds move is not always clear. A programme of analysis of stone is gradually identifying the quarries used for the manufacture of tools in Polynesia and Australia. In addition, through an extensive programme of petrological identification of Neolithic stone axes found in Europe, the sites where the stone for the axes was quarried are gradually being identified. By plotting the findspots of the axes on a map, it is clear that many of them travelled long distances from where they were made, sometimes being found in areas where a different type of stone was also being quarried for axe manufacture. Whether this pattern represents the movement of the people using the axes (an unlikely hypothesis), the exchange of gifts between adjacent groups of people, or some sort of trade probably based on a barter system, is difficult, if not impossible, to prove; but the movement of

the finds themselves cannot be disputed.

A more informative example is that of samian pottery, produced mainly in factories in France and Germany during the Roman period and exported all over the Roman Empire. From finds of coins, and from surviving Latin texts, there can be no doubt in this case that the movement of finds on such a large scale is the consequence of trade within a money-based economy. Thus, detailed study of samian pottery and other export goods can not only provide information about trade, but also about the economy of the Roman empire.

Finds also tell us about the living conditions of the site inhabitants. The amount of debris in and around a site can indicate the level of cleanliness and hygiene (or lack of it) that was prevalent-at that particular site. Care is needed in such an interpretation, however; abandoned sites can later be used by squatters or on a casual basis by travellers, so that the picture is distorted. Even without this subsequent habitation, abandoned sites attract the dumping of rubbish, and during excavation a rubbish deposit may not be distinguishable from earlier occupation layers.

The quantity of finds on a site can give an idea of the wealth of the people living there, although since most possessions would have been removed if people left the site, this too can give a distorted view. A wealthy lifestyle is likely to be reflected in a site yielding many finds of high quality; sites with few finds of a consistently poor quality suggest a relatively low standard of living. But here too there is a danger of distortion: occupants who were very poor but lived in a house with masonry foundations, surrounded by heaps of discarded food debris, and who used poor quality pottery (fragments of which would survive) might well appear to have had better living conditions than the richer occupants of a site who lived in a large timber-built house, using high-quality wooden and leather vessels (which would not usually survive), and were able to employ servants to remove debris from the immediate vicinity of the house. In the latter case it might be difficult to even prove that the building was lived in at all. In every instance, great care has to be taken when living conditions are being deduced from archaeological evidence,

since there is a real risk of misinterpretation.

When archaeologists research the way of life that people followed in the past, finds can provide direct evidence – spindle whorls, loom-weights and, in exceptional circumstances, fragments of woven cloth clearly point to the production of textiles, for example. Other indications of activity may be less direct. The analysis of wear patterns on prehistoric stone tools can show which sort of work produced a particular pattern of wear.

Organic remains provide much evidence as to how people lived in the past. Plant remains – seeds, grains, and pollens – show what species of plants and trees grew around a particular site, what plants were being deliberately cultivated, and sometimes what the plants would yield in an

ABOVE The analysis of a small sample from this clay lamp by various methods, including infra-red spectroscopy, showed that the most likely fuel used was olive oil.

RIGHT AND TOP OF THIS PAGE By studying the typology of lamps, and also by studying the manufacturers' stamps and the type of clay, the original provenance and date of the lamps can be established.

average harvest. Taken with other environmental indicators, such as land snail shells and insect remains, they also give information about the prevailing climate. And in exceptional circumstances, microscopic intestinal parasites have survived to indicate some of the health problems that people suffered.

Which animals were being hunted for food, and which were domesticated can be gleaned from the study of animal bones, and with evidence from plant and shellfish remains, there may be clues to what people ate. Attempts to establish a people's diet at any time is very difficult without supporting documentary evidence, however, as vital evidence might be missing. Because animal bones are much more likely to survive than plant remains, the evidence is unduly biased towards a meat-eating diet. And it has been well established that some animals, such as pigs, are capable of completely consuming animal bones, along with other kitchen waste, so that even the sample of animal bones from a site may not give a true picture of diet.

The excavation of archaeological sites and the study of structural remains from those sites provide a skeleton picture of life in the past. But it is the study of finds, and particularly of finds from many sites over a wide area, that fleshes out that skeleton to give a more complete picture of how people lived.

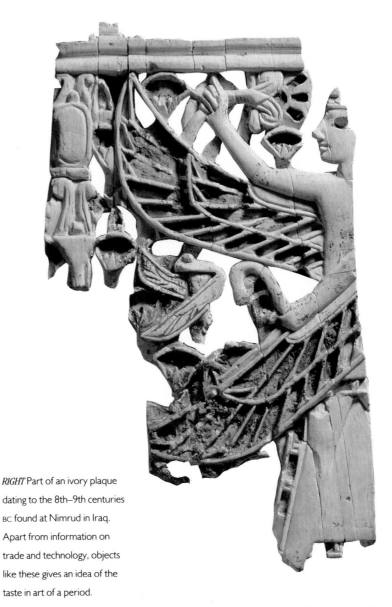

RIGHT Part of an ivory plaque dating to the 8th–9th centuries BC found at Nimrud in Iraq. Apart from information on trade and technology, objects like these gives an idea of the taste in art of a period.

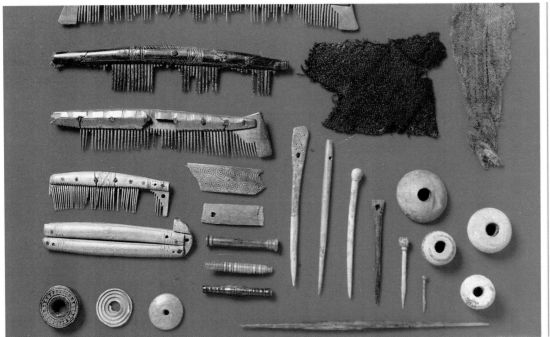

LEFT Objects such as these 10th century bone and antler combs, pins, spindle whorls and textiles can provide information about manufacturing industries and technology.

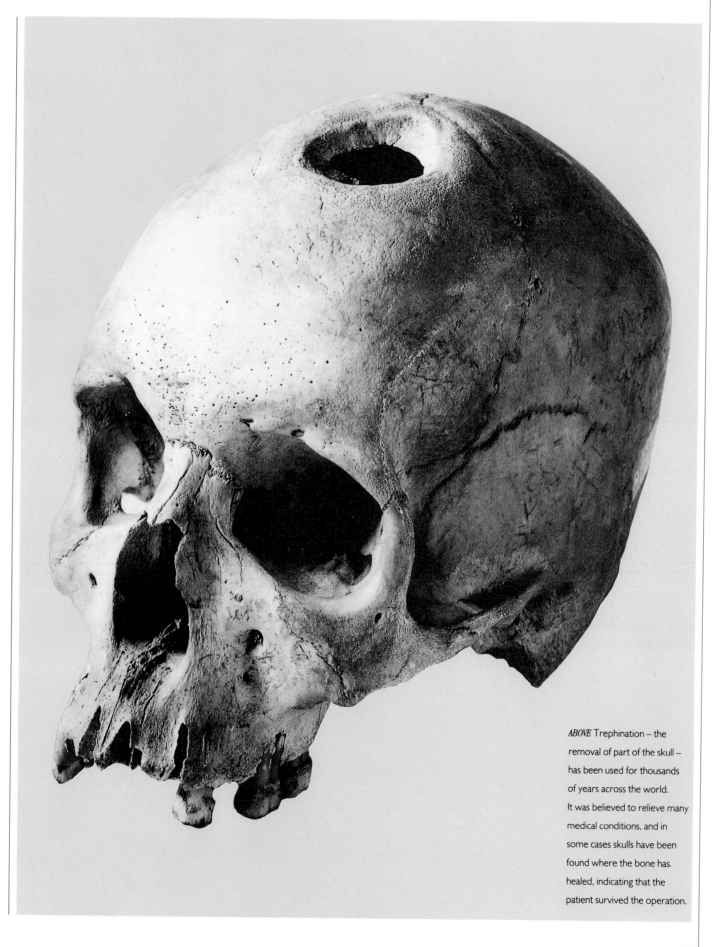

ABOVE Trephination – the removal of part of the skull – has been used for thousands of years across the world. It was believed to relieve many medical conditions, and in some cases skulls have been found where the bone has healed, indicating that the patient survived the operation.

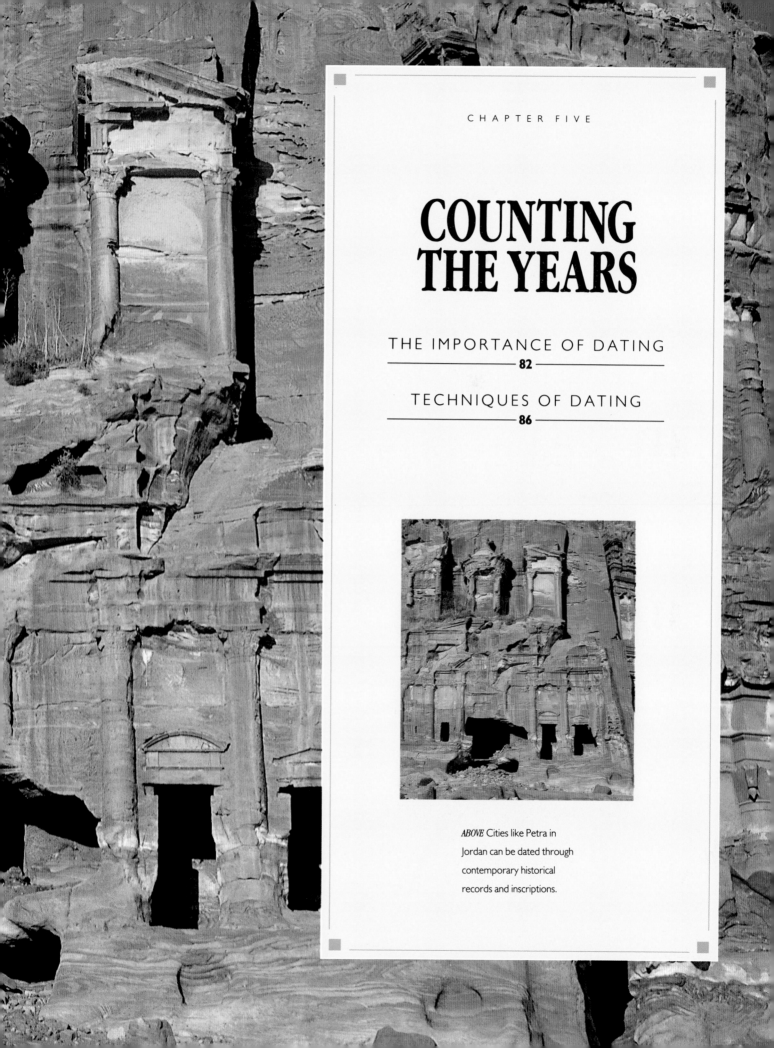

CHAPTER FIVE

COUNTING THE YEARS

THE IMPORTANCE OF DATING
82

TECHNIQUES OF DATING
86

ABOVE Cities like Petra in
Jordan can be dated through
contemporary historical
records and inscriptions.

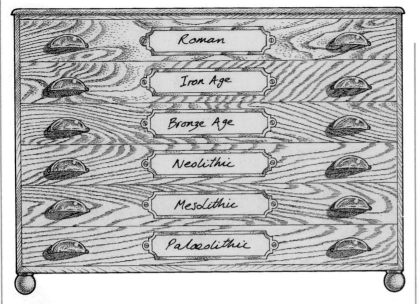

ABOVE Early systems of dating were based on the 'chest-of-drawers' system, with finds from each archaeological period in their own drawer, and no overlaps. While still loosely based on this approach, modern dating systems try to provide a continuous sequence.

FAR RIGHT Where clearly defined layers are superimposed one on top of another, it is possible to use stratigraphy for dating, a method borrowed from geology – the layers at the top are from a later period than the ones below.

■ THE IMPORTANCE OF DATING

Early antiquarians and archaeologists were greatly hampered by an almost complete lack of dating techniques for the sites and finds that they recorded and excavated. As it was difficult to know if one artefact or site was earlier or later than another, there was rarely any way of even estimating the time that had elapsed between the occupation of different sites, or parts of the same site. As more artefacts were collected and more sites discovered and excavated, the need for some method of ordering the information became more urgent, and so developed the techniques of dating.

Dating provides a vital structure for archaeological evidence; without establishing the chronological sequence in which sites were constructed, used and abandoned, it is impossible to understand the relationship between sites. While the first step towards the historical framework is establishing a sequence of events, it is also necessary to know how much time elapsed between events. A sequence and no dates is as useful as knowing that one sites lies to the west of another without knowing how far.

Apart from areas like Egypt and Mesopotamia, where very early historical records could provide dates, the first archaeologists were usually without any means of dating their sites and finds. The first moves towards dating involved the ordering of finds according to an assumed technological development: the theory was that stone tools preceded copper tools, copper tools preceded bronze tools, bronze tools preceded iron tools, and that iron tools continued in use into the historical period when dates could be obtained from written records.

This hypothethical sequence formed the basis of the Stone Age, Copper Age, Bronze Age and Iron Age system which was found to be generally accurate world-wide. Still used by archaeologists, it went only part of the way towards providing a historical framework for archaeological evidence, however. The sequence was still largely without dates, and more importantly, the development from one broad technological phase to another did not occur at the same time everywhere. While the people of one region might still be using stone tools, those in another were already using bronze for all their tools and weapons and sometimes iron as well. It gradually became clear that the technological sequence was only a broad outline – the real situation was much more complex.

Whereas intially sites were linked because they produced similar artefacts – stone tools rather than metal ones, for example – it soon became clear that there were different types of stone tools, to take just one group. Sites then began to be linked on the basis of the type of stone tools that they produced, and on some sites different types of stone tools were found in superimposed layers. Using the principles of stratigraphy, borrowed from geology, it was deduced that some types of tool were earlier than others. A network of relationships were gradually built up between different sites and finds until a sequence of events became clear. One group of sites could be seen to be more or less contemporary because they produced the same types of tool, while those which produced other types could be shown to be earlier or later in date.

The usefulness of this framework was limited, however, as the dates of occupation were known for very few sites; and furthermore, the time interval between sites and finds was also unknown. Since the framework gave no hint of the long periods of time during which tool types were in use, sites that were originally considered to be contemporary were subsequently found to be separated by hundreds or thousands of years.

LEFT On a deep site, such as in a city or tell, the many excavated layers and their relationships are very complex. It is clear from this excavation that while stratigraphy can be used for dating – for example, the modern concrete and brick structures are above the earlier levels – it has to be used very carefully, since many features cut deeply into layers below. Each layer must be carefully recorded so that the finds from each layer can be used for dating as well.

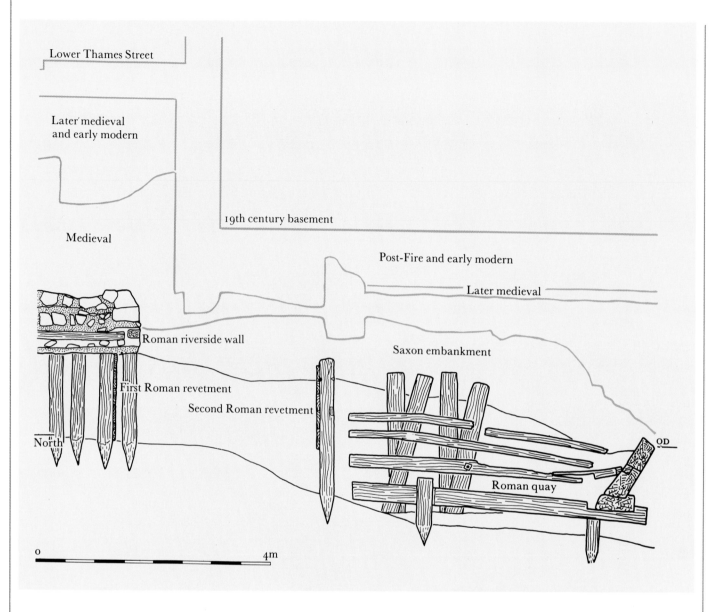

Lower Thames Street

Later medieval
and early modern

19th century basement

Medieval

Post-Fire and early modern

Later medieval

Roman riverside wall

Saxon embankment

First Roman revetment

Second Roman revetment

North

OD

Roman quay

0   4m

ABOVE Particularly on deep sites, stratigraphy is employed as an overall means of dating layers, since layers at the top of a site are usually found to be later in date than ones beneath. This shows clearly in the sequence of deposits along the edge of the River Thames in London.

Dates had to be obtained for many of the sites before the historical sequence would become clearer.

The only way to solve the problem of obtaining precise dates is to devise methods of dating sites and finds accurately. The search for such dating methods has continued for some time, but in the second half of this century several methods have been developed, which provide much better ways of dating some sites and finds. These have dramatically altered and of course improved archaeologists' knowledge about the duration of various episodes within pre-history, and it now seems possible that archaeology, and particularly prehistoric archaeology, will eventually have a dated historical sequence as clear as that used by historians.

TECHNIQUES OF DATING

Some of the earliest techniques of dating were originally developed by the Swedish archaeologist Oscar Montelius (1843–1921) in the late 19th century. Although they have been modified since then, his techniques using finds still form the mainstay of most dating programmes.

The principles of stratigraphy, originally borrowed from geology, are based on the fact that where a succession of undisturbed layers are found one on top of the other, the layers below will be earlier in date than those above. Under these ideal conditions, stratigraphy provides a sequence that can be converted into a

time-scale if the individual layers themselves can be dated. Unfortunately, such undisturbed layers are relatively rare on archaeological sites – most layers have suffered some later disturbance from a number of causes (even burrowing animals or tree roots), so that an assessment of the integrity of each layer has to be made. The movement of earthworms throughout layers can also cause a great deal of disruption, blurring the divisions.

Where similar finds are consistently found in layers dated to the same period of time, it can be assumed that these finds belong to that time period. And likewise, finds of that period found in a layer which is otherwise undated can help to date that layer. If a group of finds whose date is known is found with others of unknown date, it is likely that all the finds are contemporary, although if this association of finds happens only once, doubt lingers about its accuracy. Finds can also be dated from historical sources. Coins often carry inscriptions linking them to the reign of a particular ruler, or in some cases, a particular year; other finds found with such coins can be dated by association.

Using these techniques, a network of links between many finds and archaeological layers (contexts) form a dated framework used to date other finds and contexts. The result is often a very useful skeleton history of the region, but one which is constantly undergoing revision and correction as new information is discovered. Such networks are inevitably built up on a regional basis because the finds are usually confined to a

limited geographical region. Those that were traded over wide geographical areas, though, can be useful in linking the dating frameworks of different regions. Once such a framework has been established, the emphasis is on finding new methods of dating finds and ways of refining existing methods to increase accuracy.

One method of dating finds is by the use of typology, the importance of which was demonstrated by Pitt-Rivers. Typology is the study of the development of particular types of artefact over a period of time. The shape of a storage pot, for example, does not remain static – as copies are made, tiny errors inadvertently change its shape – so that after many such consecutive copies, the pot's shape may appear significantly different from the first one. If the style of the pot is delib-

ABOVE TOP Typology is the study of the development of artefacts of the same type to build up a dated sequence. Here the earliest type of axe is of stone (on the left), which were superseded by copper and bronze ones.

ABOVE Finds can often be dated by manufacturers' stamps (as antiques are often dated today). This is the base of a samian pot, and the potter's stamp can be dated to the 2nd century AD.

LEFT The dates obtained through radiocarbon dating can often be refined by calibrating them with dates obtained by other means. One such method is to compare the dates with those obtained by dendrochronology, especially from the extremely long-lived tree, the bristlecone pine.

erately changed when it is copied, particularly if the decoration is being changed to keep up with current fashion, the differences between earlier and later pots are even more noticeable. It was recognized that groups of artefacts, such as pots, could be arranged in a sequence according to these changes. If some of the artefacts could then be precisely dated, a dating framework could be established.

Seriation, a development of typology, is a method of putting groups of objects into chronological order on the basis of similarities and differences. In this way, specific dates can be given to a sequence of finds as more information becomes available: if, for example, a cemetery which had been in use for several decades is excavated, the finds from each grave are studied as individual groups to be fitted into an overall sequence. This method of dating has certain difficulties however. The methods of excavation have to be extremely rigorous, and putting the finds into a dated sequence often relies heavily on individual judgement, although statistical techniques and computers are nowadays used to handle and control the data.

Although many sites and finds are still excavated, analysed and dated by the sorting of finds, and so on (methods which are never likely to be completely replaced), numerous scientific methods of dating have now been developed.

The earliest, and still the best-known, modern scientific dating method was radiocarbon dating, also known as carbon 14 (or C14) dating. Perhaps its most important aspect is that it is not confined to a particular region. It can be used to date finds from anywhere in the world and so offers a means of comparing dated finds from different regions.

Radiocarbon dating works by analysing the ratios of the various isotopes of carbon in a sample of organic material, and can only be used, therefore, on organic remains such as wood, charcoal and bone. It has been recently used to date the Turin Shroud, previously believed to have wrapped the body of Christ, to the medieval period. Carbon 14 is a radioactive isotope of carbon that is absorbed by all living things; the proportion of carbon 14 to other isotopes of carbon remains constant, but when something dies, the carbon 14 in it decays at a known rate, while the other isotopes stay the same. Thus, by measuring the proportions of the carbon isotopes in an organic sample, the age of the sample can be calculated.

FAR LEFT Excavated graves can be dated by stratigraphy, by scientific dating of the bones (such as by carbon 14 dating), by the type of finds present as grave goods, and sometimes by historical records. This Sumerian burial in northern Iraq has been dated to about 2000 BC.

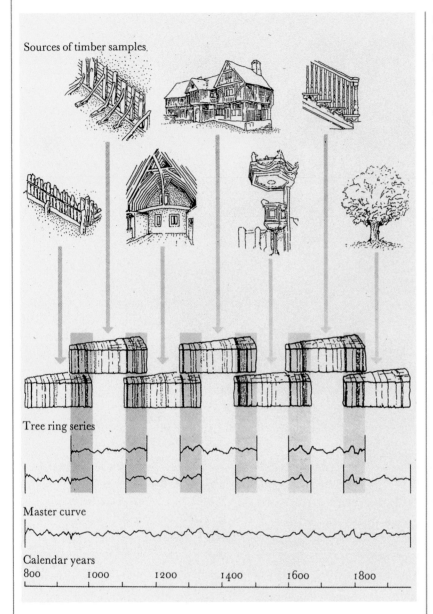

Sources of timber samples.

Tree ring series

Master curve

Calendar years
800   1000   1200   1400   1600   1800

ABOVE The method of dating using tree-rings (dendrochronology) involves taking samples from timbers of different ages, and linking them together to provide an overall dating sequence.

But several factors affect the accuracy of radiocarbon dating. Initially assumed that the level of carbon 14 in the environment that was available to be absorbed by living things remained at a constant level, subsequent research has shown that the amount of carbon 14 varies, possibly as a result of sunspot activity. Some of the dates that have been obtained are therefore misleading, making the sample appear younger or older than it really is.

A second problem is that the calculation of the half-life of carbon 14 is still being refined. (The half-life of a radioactive isotope is the time it takes for half of the radioactivity to disappear as the isotope decays). For carbon 14, the half-life is approximately 5,730 years, but since this is

a crucial quantity in the calculation of any radiocarbon date, the more accurate it is, the more accurate the date will be. At the time the first radiocarbon dates were calculated, the half-life was thought to be around 5,568 years, and so early dates have had to be corrected.

Tests of the accuracy of radiocarbon dates against samples of wood dated by dendrochronology (see below) have shown that 'radiocarbon years' cannot always be directly equated with calendar years (because the amount of carbon 14 varies), so that a date of 4,100 BC in 'radiocarbon years' may actually be closer to a real date of 5,000 BC. To correct this error radiocarbon dates are calibrated by studying the difference between radiocarbon dates and tree-ring dates. For the later range of radiocarbon dates this calibration is well-established. The tree-ring dates are obtained from samples of extremely long-lived trees, such as the bristlecone pine. These trees grow in the south-west of the United States, and some are over 4,000 years old.

Because of the difficulties associated with radiocarbon dating, each new date is given a statistical margin of error. A date of 3220 BC ±100 indicates a 68% chance that the real date lies within 100 years either side of 3220 BC, and a 95% chance that it will lie within 200 years either side of that date. Despite all these problems, radiocarbon dating has revolutionized the study of archaeology. It has often provided dates where there was previously no method of dating available at all, and for many periods, accuracy to the nearest century or so is far better than produced by previous dating methods. Other methods of dating based on similar principles of measuring the balance between decaying and stable isotopes are being developed, and these may well become as important as radiocarbon dating.

Dendrochronology, also called tree-ring dating, is not only used for calibrating radiocarbon dates, but also for providing accurate dates for old timbers. It relies on the fact that trees grow annual rings, and that in some trees the thickness of these rings is subject to seasonal variation; when a tree is felled, a pattern of annual rings of varying thickness can be seen. By matching the patterns of tree rings from trees of known dates, a larger pattern of thick and thin

rings covering hundreds or even thousands of years can be built up. If the pattern of rings from a piece of undated timber is matched against a dated pattern, the piece can also be dated.

Not all types of tree provide a good pattern of tree rings, however. Patterns can be affected by climate, which varies from region to region, so that a particular tree-ring pattern established in one area cannot be used for dating timbers from another part of the world. In fact timbers rarely survive to be discovered on archaeological sites, and when they do they are not always in good enough condition to be used for dating; furthermore, if they were part of timber structures and had been shaped, not enough of the ring pattern may survive. And even if a structural timber can be dated, there is always the possibility that it was stored for some time between being felled and being used, or even that it was re-used timber salvaged from an earlier building. But these problems notwithstanding, tree-ring dating is extremely useful, and can provide dates accurate to the nearest year.

Thermoluminescence dating, usually abbreviated to TL dating, is used for ceramic artefacts, such as pottery. This method is based on the fact that mineral crystals accumulate and store energy, which is released when they are heated. All clay contains such minerals, and when pottery is fired, the energy stored in the crystals is released as light. From then on, the crystals continue to accumulate and store energy. By heating a sample

ABOVE Where wood survives (usually in waterlogged conditions), it can be dated by carbon 14 dating or more usually by cutting slices from the timbers with a saw, and dating them by their tree-rings.

ABOVE Taking samples of burnt clay for dating by archaeomagnetic dating.

of pottery and measuring the amount of energy released, the time that has elapsed since the pot was last fired (usually when the pot was made) can be calculated. As with all dating methods, there are drawbacks. Not all the energy released on heating comes from the crystals, since some will be from radioactivity absorbed from the soil, and different types of crystal vary in their ability to absorb energy. These things have to be taken into consideration when calculating dates, but the method is nonetheless valuable. It can also be used on some burnt stone tools, and is particularly useful if such tools were heated during their manufacture.

Other methods of dating that are useful in specific cases include archaeomagnetic dating, used to date ceramic materials that have not been moved since they were last heated, such as the clay floor of a pottery kiln or a hearth inside a hut or house. Clay retains a record of the intensity and direction of the earth's magnetic field when it was last fired, because on heating the magnetic oxides in the clay align with the prevailing magnetic field. The earth's magnetic field changes in strength and direction over time, and by measuring the local magnetic field around the clay, an estimate of when the clay was last fired can be calculated.

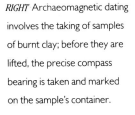

RIGHT Archaeomagnetic dating involves the taking of samples of burnt clay; before they are lifted, the precise compass bearing is taken and marked on the sample's container.

With the range of scientific dating methods now available, archaeologists are better equipped than ever before to construct a reliable sequence of dates. But for many, scientific methods of dating are still very expensive in relation to the resources available. Unfortunately, dating by such methods is still rare.

No matter what the means of obtaining a date, care still has to be taken in assessing what it means. Having a date accurate to within one year for a piece of timber is a pointless exercise if the relationship of that timber to other finds and to the site as a whole is unknown. An object of a particular date in a particular context does not automatically mean that it dates that context: a context often contains artefacts of quite different dates, and it is the archaeologists's task to arrive at an interpretation that fits all the facts.

PUTTING TOGETHER THE PIECES

ABOVE An imaginative
impression of the construction
of a Roman quay based on
excavated evidence.

Ronald Embleton

■ WHAT HAPPENS TO SITES AND FINDS

Even when excavations are featured in newspaper articles and television programmes, archaeological sites are rarely in the public eye for more than a very short while. Once the excavation is over, the vast majority of sites revert to the anonymity that they possessed before it started. In most cases, there are insufficient surviving remains to make it worthwhile conserving the site for public display: if it has been fully excavated, all that may remain to be seen are, literally, a few depressions in the natural subsoil, even if what was excavated above was quite spectacular. Most sites do not produce remains that can be readily understood by casual visitors, and they often consist of little more than holes in the ground showing where posts once formed part of a timber building, pits dug for various purposes, or ditches for drainage, boundaries and defence. Such holes cannot be 'conserved', and displaying such a site to the public would require considerable reconstruction.

The choice as to whether the remains of a site are preserved for public display depends both on there being suitable remains, but also on a suitable site and finance. Nowadays, most excavations are conducted on sites that are about to be destroyed, and so when the excavation is finished, the site is left to its fate. Although in some cases, part of the site may survive because it lies outside the area to be destroyed, more

BELOW Before this building on the banks of the River Thames in London was constructed, the site was excavated; it produced important evidence of a Roman quay (see reconstruction on the previous page).

LEFT At times it may be possible to conserve or reconstruct a site, by incorporating it in the development plans. This site was once that of an ancient meeting place mound; it was partly excavated, and the mound reconstructed as part of the landscaping design.

often the whole site disappears and only excavation records and finds are left.

But in some cases, the remains unearthed by excavation are sufficiently important and interesting to be worth displaying. If the site is not in danger of being destroyed, it may be possible to raise funds to conserve the site for display, and the way the site is presented depends largely on the nature of the remains: the ruins of an Islamic mosque for example, may need the walls to be strengthened and made safe, and suitable access provided in order to view the remains. More fragile sites often need to be roofed over or be completely enclosed in order to prevent their deterioration. On the rare occasions when a site due to be destroyed is found to be very important, construction plans may be changed to accommodate the display of the site, or the remains might be moved to somewhere where they can be preserved, displayed, and enjoyed by the public.

Many sites where archaeological remains are on public display have never been fully excavated, and any further excavations on these sites are usually undertaken to add to the information on display. Some sites may have their own museums, but in most instances, finds from any excavations are kept in local and national museums.

Since museums can display very few of the objects that they hold, most of the finds held by museums are in permanent storage. While some of these are not suitable for display, many others are not seen because a better example is already on display. The importance of these stored finds is that they form a research collection available for study by archaeologists and others, and some are used for travelling and temporary exhibitions, and in teaching collections on loan to schools.

At some exceptional sites it has been necessary to reconstruct part of the site and the finds for display in order that they should be fully understood by visitors. The most dramatic example of this is the Jorvik Centre in York, which has a lifelike reconstruction of part of York in the Viking age (complete with sounds and smells), a reconstruction of the excavation itself, and a display of finds. Dynamic displays such as this make sites and finds more comprehensible, and are likely to be increasingly used at excavation sites and within museums in the future.

■ WHY INTERPRETATION IS NECESSARY

Unlike historical documents, archaeological sites and their finds do not tell us anything directly. To gain information from sites and finds, they have to be treated as evidence, and information has to be deduced from them in much the same way as a detective uses forensic evidence. As has been

Some sites are so important that it may be necessary for a rescue operation on an international scale.

ABOVE Many important Nubian monuments were threatened by flooding due to the construction of the Aswan dam.

RIGHT After they were recorded, these monuments at Abu Simbel were dismantled and reassembled out of reach of the floodwaters.

shown, during the excavation itself, every decision by an excavator in distinguishing one layer or context from another is a form of interpretation. In post-excavation analysis, groups of contexts are interpreted as representing walls, postholes, filled-in pits and ditches, and so on, before being put together as clues to structures such as buildings and fences. The process is similar to doing a jigsaw puzzle, but without a clear pattern on each piece.

Except in rare cases, a similar analysis has to be applied to finds as these have no inscriptions or written records to identify them. Once they have been dated, though, their significance for the site where they were found still requires interpretation. For example, a Neolithic stone axe found in a pit inside a Roman building might be interpreted as a stray find unconnected with the Roman structure. If the building is thought to be a temple, however, the stone axe may well be interpreted as having been picked up by someone and deliberately buried within the temple in the Roman period as an offering to the gods.

The other major factor that makes interpretation necessary is the problem of accidental survival. On most sites, for instance, foundations alone survive, making it impossible to establish the complete height or appearance of buildings. Both for sites and for finds, the greatest problems are caused by the fact that organic materials rarely survive. For example, in most parts of the world, wood has been used extensively for building, fuel, tools, and even machinery, yet only in exceptional circumstances does wood survive. As a result, archaeologists need to use a great deal of interpretation to fill in the gaps in the evidence caused by the accidental survival of some remains while others have perished. With thorough analysis, archaeological sites and finds can yield a great deal of evidence, and with skilled interpretation as well, much meaningful information can result.

■ METHODS OF INTERPRETATION

There are many techniques of archaeological interpretation, and several layers at which interpretation is necessary, from sorting out the structural sequence of excavated buildings to assessing the place of a nation in world history. At each level, there are broad approaches that are nearly always used as the basis of interpretation.

The most basic level of interpreting archaeological remains is during the post-excavation work, when the contexts are analysed and, where possible, dated and fitted together. As we have seen, this involves a considerable sorting of data in order to build up a picture of the site – to see, for example, what buildings existed there, and at what periods. The result is an approximate history of the site: for example, the site may begin with the construction of a farmhouse with a few outbuildings, then a large barn was built, alterations were made to the farmhouse, two of the outbuildings were demolished, and so on.

On a site with good dating evidence for most contexts and easily established relationships between them, such an interpretation is relatively

straightforward. On some sites, though, the dating may be too imprecise to be of particular value, and may lack direct relationships between the features. For example, a site may consist largely of a number of postholes, all dating to the Neolithic period. It may be obvious that the postholes represent structures, but little else may be immediately apparent. In this situation, it is possible to try to group the postholes with similar characteristics, such as depth, diameter, and so on, and then to see if patterns of similar postholes reveal likely structures, such as circular or rectangular buildings. This method of analysis does not always work, and sometimes interpretation of such sites is little better than guesswork.

BELOW It is not feasible to put most finds from excavations on public display. Instead, they are housed in storerooms in museums to be used by researchers.

LEFT Excavations are usually carried out on sites scheduled for development, so that the archaeological evidence can never be displayed on the site. The excavation of the Viking site at York was so important, though, that the development plans were changed.

RIGHT The evidence from the site and the excavation itself has been reconstructed in a very vivid way at the Jorvik Viking centre, and is a very popular attraction for visitors from all over the world. This scene shows an evening meal being prepared in a 10th century Viking household.

The interpretation of individual sites is then followed by that of the archaeology of a particular region, studying all the relevant sites and finds to assess how they relate to each other. Specific studies of a region may have already been carried out, perhaps on the trade in a particular type of pottery, or on defended hilltop sites. The interpretation of a region's archaeology therefore involves both the raw data from sites and finds, and also secondary information from previous specific studies.

At its widest level, the interpretation of archaeology on a world-wide basis almost always relies on secondary sources. Many global studies of specific aspects of archaeology have been done, as have those linking several regions. Even using secondary sources alone, the amount of information involved is usually too great to be encompassed by a single person, and so of necessity such studies are often undertaken as a team project. Alternatively, the volume of data can be restricted by selecting a specific archaeological

period or group of periods – the study might be confined to prehistoric archaeology world-wide, for example. For both regional and world-wide studies, archaeological interpretation is based more on an assessment of evidence and arguments put forward by other archaeologists than

ABOVE The site and reconstruction of the Minoan palace at Knossos, Crete.

ABOVE The excavated site of a temple of Mithras, on Hadrian's Wall, England, on display to the public.

an assessment of primary data. Although at a regional level it is often possible to check secondary sources against the original data, this is impossible globally. Nevertheless, the general approach is broadly the same, working with small groups of data and finding links between them in an attempt to build up a coherent picture of the past. This underlines the need for rigorous recording and interpretation by every member of an archaeological team on individual excavations, since ultimately the information may be used in a worldwide study.

It is essential for archaeologists to approach their subject without personal or political prejudice, since past and present governments have not been averse to misusing archaeological data for nationalistic purposes. Biased interpretations have now and again been put forward as propaganda to promote a country or political or religious ideologies.

■ THE FRONTIERS OF INTERPRETATION

Quite apart from the problems caused by differing survival rates for different materials (depending on the materials and the conditions), and by insufficient dating evidence, archaeological interpretation is limited by the nature of the evidence itself. Consisting of material remains – objects, buildings and other structures – there are limits as to how much can be deduced from such evidence about the people who used them.

In any general interpretation of archaeological evidence, whether of a particular site, region, or world-wide, four main themes of information recur. In descending order of reliability, these are technological information, economic information, social information, and information about religions.

Technological information is the most reliably deduced information. For example, the constituents of bronze used in the manufacture of bronze tools can be scientifically analysed to gain information on ancient metallurgy. Furthermore, it is often possible to replicate the artefacts in order to test the hypotheses about a particular object, although in some cases several different technological methods might arrive at an identical end-product.

Economic information is not normally capable of being tested in the same way, but is still fairly reliable as the economy is so closely associated with material evidence. By studying evidence for transport, coinage, agriculture and the trade of objects, a great deal can be assessed about the economy in a particular period. Many of these factors can be deduced or estimated from surviving archaeological evidence, but other factors – such as size of population, whether farming is only at subsistence level or is producing a surplus, and if so, how large a surplus – are much more difficult to assess. Consequently, the interpretation of ancient economies is very complex.

Information about social organization is even more difficult to deduce from archaeological evidence. Although studies of modern societies show that there are usually strong links between social organization and material objects, these links are not the same in every society. Whereas in one, an iron axehead may be a tool used for woodworking and cutting down trees, in another it may be a unit of value – a cow might be worth two axeheads, for example. In a third society, the axehead may be a symbol of authority, only possessed by certain people. But while axeheads from different societies may perform widely differing social functions, the axeheads themselves may be almost identical. Archaeolo-

ABOVE A museum reconstruction of the temple of Mithras, on Hadrian's Wall, England.

ABOVE Experiments can be done to find out how ditches silt up over long periods of time, how earthworks erode, and how finds move. Such information helps archaeologists to interpret excavated evidence more accurately.

gists might be able to distinguish between them, but without other evidence, such as inscriptions or historical documents, the axes will not reveal their differing social roles.

The same is true when assessing evidence about political matters. The excavation of a village may reveal a number of small buildings clustered around one much larger building. Even with evidence for the level of wealth in each building, this could imply that the village society was led by a single chief, who lived in the biggest house in the centre of the village, or that the village was run by a council of all the members of the village, who built a large central hall in which to hold their meetings.

But it is information about ancient religions which is the most difficult to derive with any certainty from archaeological evidence. Many ordinary everyday objects and buildings could have been used for religious purposes, but this would not be detectable from archaeological evidence alone. It might be obvious that an object had a religious purpose, but often even this is debatable: a small, crudely carved wooden figure might be the cult statue of a god, but it could equally well be a child's toy. Often, even when

an object can be positively identified as having religious significance, it may have no bearing on the situation in which it was found – many looted religious objects have been found in places far from where they were made and used. Since the only link between religion and material objects is through ritual, it is difficult to use archaeological evidence to find out about ancient religions. Without written evidence, it is impossible to know the wider significance of rituals, even if the cult objects used in the religion are known, let alone the actual beliefs of the people.

ARCHAEOLOGICAL EXPERIMENTS

Experiments are a crucial part of archaeological interpretation. Used to test theories and interpretations relating to technology and subsistence, experiments can also test the very basic interpretations that are carried out during the course of an excavation: whether or not a hole in the ground functioned as a pit or a posthole, what a particular pit was used for, and so on. As it checks the very evidence from which all archaeological

LEFT Experiments to investigate how pottery was made and fired are frequently carried out.

BELOW The remains of kilns after the firing experiment can be analysed and excavated to be compared with excavated examples.

RIGHT A variety of possible reconstruction can often be done using the same evidence. This building is a possible reconstruction of a timber house, based on the results from excavation.

BELOW The same evidence has been used for this house, but the reconstruction is quite different.

interpretation is derived, this basic experimentation is the most important, although the least spectacular.

Experiments that are used fall into three main categories: those which examine how archaeological sites are formed and how finds decay; those which see how finds functioned, and with what degree of efficiency; and those to test interpretations of how structures were built. The dividing line between experiments and reconstructions is often narrow, because finds and structures have to be reconstructed in order to undertake experiments.

It is of the utmost importance to see how sites decay and how they appear when they are excavated, and these were the earliest type of experiment to be conducted. Pitt-Rivers studied the processes involved when ditches were abandoned and silted up, and the broad conclusions that he reached have been verified by later experiments. By digging ditches and placing objects in them and in the surrounding soils, it is possible to assess how finds move and become mixed as the sides of the ditch weather and collapse inwards, carrying the finds with them. Marker poles can be used to check the depth of silting, and by excavating parts of the ditch at intervals, the rate of silting can be assessed. Unfortunately, once the initial silting has taken place, the weathering of the ditch is very slow, and such experiments need to run for a period of over a hundred years to gain the maximum results.

The material dug from a ditch was often used to construct an associated mound or bank,

LEFT Reconstructions of sites, such as this crannog, can be tourist attractions, but they can also be used as experiments in showing how sites were constructed and how they appear when destroyed and excavated.

and so some experimental ditches have been dug in conjunction with the construction of experimental mounds. While ditches become filled with silt over time, mounds are gradually flattened by weathering, and if a mound is adjacent to a ditch, this will affect the pattern of silting in the ditch. Climatic conditions and the underlying subsoil also affect the pattern of decay on sites; sand, for example, weathers more rapidly than chalk. There is a great deal of scope for such experiments, but as yet relatively few experiments have been conducted.

Experiments are also done to examine other features found during excavation. Iron Age storage pits, for example, have been reconstructed and tested, showing that if constructed correctly and properly sealed, grain can be successfully stored in such pits without spoiling; another experiment shows how different methods of erecting a timber post cause differently shaped postholes. Because of the huge variation in archaeological sites, and the features found on them, many more experiments of this nature need to be done, and comparisons between them made, before the accuracy of interpretations of excavated features can be reliably accepted.

Another type of experiment involves the reconstruction of finds: experiments on stone tools, for example, have greatly increased knowledge about how they were used and what they were used for. By making copies of prehistoric stone implements and then using the copies to cut, scrape and chop different materials (such as growing crops, bones and hides), the patterns of wear formed by these processes can be matched to wear patterns on the original artefacts.

Stone axes have been used in several experiments to find out the method and efficiency of hafting, and to see how efficient they were in felling trees. The marks left behind on the wood have also been studied for comparison with excavated pieces of timber, and similar experiments have been used to investigate the use of bronze and iron axes.

Making copies is one way of discovering how objects were originally manufactured. One of the most common experiments of this kind is making and firing of pottery, which not only tests methods of pottery construction, decoration, glazing, and firing methods, but also leaves the remains of the kiln itself which can be compared with excavated examples. Because various types

RIGHT Reconstructions of finds are often done so that they can be better understood, studied and recorded, and also so that they are more meaningful when put on display. It is essential, though, to ensure that the reconstructed parts of an object are easily distinguishable, as in this restored anthropomorphic jar from Lachish, Israel, dating to around 1200–1000 BC.

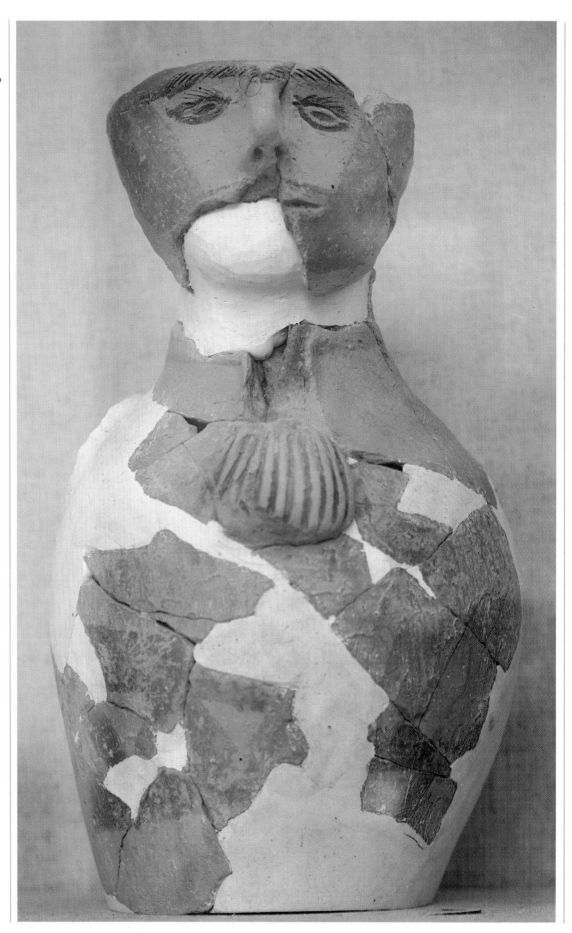

The largest of the mission churches at Pecos Pueblo, ca. 1625.
La iglesia más grande de la misión de Pecos, ca. 1625.

of kiln and pottery were in use at different times, many experiments of this type are needed, and similar tests can be used to investigate the manufacture of tiles, and the smelting of ores, for example.

But the most spectacular experiments involve full-size reconstruction of buildings and other structures. Most experiments of this type have so far concentrated on investigating timber buildings with posts set in postholes, because these are usually the most difficult structures to interpret during excavation. Timber houses of several different periods and cultures have been reconstructed in various experiments, leading to a much better understanding of how such buildings were originally built. Experiments have been taken still further, to see how such buildings functioned through use, and in some cases have been left to decay and fall down, or have been burnt down, in order to compare the resulting remains with excavated evidence.

Best-known to the general public perhaps, are experiments where reconstructions of early boats and ships have been used to follow and thus test the feasibility of migration routes which might have been used by ancient people, such as

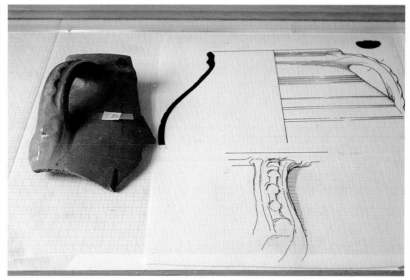

the experiments conducted by Thor Heyerdahl. Watercraft have also been reconstructed to test how they were manufactured and how well they functioned, as in the recent case of *Olympias*, a reconstructed Greek trireme.

Although fundamental to many aspects of interpretation, archaeological experiments are only now being accepted as an essential branch of research, and there is still a great deal of work to be done in all spheres.

ABOVE TOP This reconstruction drawing is exhibited close to the ruins of a mission church in Pecos Pueblo, New Mexico.

ABOVE As long as the circumference of part of a pottery vessel can be established, it is possible to do reconstruction drawings.

ABOVE An aerial view of a medieval castle at Totnes, England.

ABOVE RIGHT An artist's impression, based on archaeological evidence, of how the castle may have appeared in the 14th century.

ARCHAEOLOGICAL RECONSTRUCTIONS

Apart from those used in archaeological experiments, reconstructions mainly show what sites and finds were like when they were in use. The majority of archaeological finds are broken, damaged or decayed, and it is usually difficult to envisage what a site looked like in its heyday by simply looking at the excavated remains.

Artefacts are frequently reconstructed before they are put on display, which may involve little more than repair work, such as sticking pieces of pot together and filling any remaining gaps. In other cases, however, a complete reconstruction of an object is put on display alongside the remains of the original, which may be corroded or damaged. These reconstructions are often made of the organic elements of a composite implement: a reconstructed wooden shaft might be fitted to a bronze spearhead to give a better impression of its original appearance.

As well as physical reconstructions, drawings and paintings can be used to portray views of sites and finds. Drawings of objects published as research data for use by archaeologists frequently incorporate an element of reconstruction, but this should be clearly distinguishable from the surviving portions of the object. For drawings for display, however, this distinction is usually omitted since the purpose of the drawing is to give an overall impression of the original object. Such drawings can be displayed alongside the surviving remains of the object.

Drawings and paintings are mainly used to portray an archaeological site at a particular point in time. Such representations have to be very carefully researched, ensuring that as far as possible every detail is correct. Even so, there is often insufficient evidence to portray the whole site in detail, and artists need to use their imaginations to fill these details in.

Even with the cost of detailed research, a set of reconstruction drawings of a site is usually far cheaper than a physical reconstruction; in any

LEFT It is usually easier to build a model rather than a full-size reconstruction, and yet this can still give a realistic impression of a site.

ABOVE Re-enactments of battles and the use of replicas of the armour and weapons of past armies for displays is a popular pursuit, and can lead to new ideas about equipment and methods of warfare.

case, such detailed drawings are generally needed as preparation for a physical reconstruction. Drawings can often give views of the site that are difficult or impossible to achieve with a physical reconstruction, such as aerial or cutaway views, showing both the interior and exterior of a building at the same time. Apart from their use for research, such reconstruction drawings and paintings are used for display purposes for site visitors, and are often published as illustrations in books and magazines. This type of illustration is not confined to buildings, but is also used for structures such as bridges, frontier defences, ships, and even for people. It can be used to show almost anything, from what an object looked like to how it was made, how it was used and how it was found.

A method of reconstruction which incorporates some of the advantages of both physical reconstruction and reconstruction drawings is the scale model. Such models of sites and structures have the advantage of giving a three-dimensional view and show the site in its entirety. Models too can be constructed to give a view of both the interior and exterior of a structure. Their only problem is that they do not convey the feeling and atmosphere of a site and often appear less authentic than a skilful reconstruction drawing.

Full-scale life-size reconstructions give visitors the best idea of what the site was like in the past, however. Often these are constructed in the open air, on or near the site that produced the archaeological evidence on which they were based. This is particularly true of buildings where both the structure of the building itself and its relationship to other buildings on the site are important. Sites that have extensive ruins open to the public sometimes have one part reconstructed in order to convey an idea of how the whole site may have once appeared.

There are sites where it is not only possible to visit and see the reconstructions, but also to take part in activities simulating the way people lived on that site in the past, or even to live there for several days to get some sort of impression of the way of life.

An alternative to this type of full-scale reconstruction is the type of reconstruction used at the Jorvik Centre in York, where special effects, including sounds and smells, give visitors an impression of what it was like to walk through York in the Viking era. In future, modern technology is likely to be increasingly used in ways like this, presenting the results of archaeological research in a form that can be readily understood. Future technology is a more real and more easily grasped way to present the past, and as such presentation becomes more widely used, more and more people will come to realize what archaeologists and historians have known for so long – that the past is the key to the future.

ABOVE Restoration of a temple being carried out at Petra. Before such restorations take place, it is essential that the remains of the structures are fully recorded.

LEFT Part of the vivid life-size reconstruction at the Jorvik Viking Centre in York.

WHAT NEXT?

ABOVE Visitors at the partly restored site of Ephesus, Turkey.

■ WHAT TO DO IF YOU WANT TO KNOW MORE

Whatever approach you wish to follow, the first step is to visit your local library. This will usually have a selection of archaeological books, and will probably have details of archaeological societies in the locality, and any extra-mural courses that are available. Even if the library does not have the information that you need, the librarian will probably be able to tell you where you can find it: with hundreds of books available about all aspects of archaeology, it is as well to sample a few of these to get a better idea of what aspects of archaeology interest you most of all. There is a selection of books listed at the end of this book, but this is just the tip of the iceberg.

LEFT More and more museums are being established every year. In this open-air museum, the buildings themselves are part of the overall display.

BELOW There are also many more indoor museums with a wealth of varied displays.

Visiting sites and museums is another good way of finding out about archaeology, and general guide books to archaeological sites and museums that are open to the public are available for many regions. These give times when the sites are open and how to find them, along with a short description of the site or museums. Tourist organizations also have information about archaeological sites and museums, and will have details of any events taking place at sites – reconstructions of past battles, displays, and demonstrations of ancient crafts, to name but a few.

Many people find it worthwhile to join an archaeological society. Such societies usually

ABOVE Archaeologists are becoming more aware of the need to provide access on excavations for tourists, local people and for representatives of the funding bodies.

BELOW There are a variety of lectures offered by museums and archaeological societies, both in the lunchtime and in the evenings.

offer a programme of lectures on a range of archaeological subjects, excursions to archaeological sites, and sometimes other activities such as the chance to participate in fieldwork or excavation. Some have their own libraries of archaeological books for use by their members, usually containing a much wider range than are held by public libraries or are available in bookshops.

In many areas, it is possible to enrol for adult education classes in archaeology. These are often run by university extra-mural departments as evening classes (although daytime courses are held in some areas), and the range of courses on offer tends to depend on the lecturers that are available – introductory and basic courses are popular and are quite frequently held. Most courses are for education and enjoyment only, and do not lead to a qualification, but some courses lead to a diploma, and many universities offer part-time and full-time degree courses in archaeology.

Once you have made the first step towards finding out more about archaeology, it is likely that you will never turn back.

■ WHAT TO DO IF YOU FIND SOMETHING

Many archaeological sites and finds are discovered by people as they are going about their everyday work. Although many go unrecognized, stray finds are more commonly discovered than sites, and every one is potentially important, adding to archaeological evidence, and perhaps leading to the discovery of a new site. The ownership of archaeological finds depends on the local laws (in some countries all archaeological artefacts are automatically the property of the state and have to be reported, while in others the finds belong to the owner of the land on which they were found), but whatever the ownership, each find needs to be properly recorded if it is to be of any use archaeologically.

If an archaeological find is discovered, a detailed record of the circumstances of the discovery and the exact findspot should be compiled. This should be accurate enough for the findspot to be plotted on a map and for someone else to be able to find the location. Then report the find to an appropriate authority – a local museum is usually a good starting point, since it may employ an archaeologist. If there is no local museum, there may be a professional archaeologist in the area, perhaps working for the local authority. Either of these should be able to advise on the importance of the find and what to do next, but if there is no one in the area, the local reference library should be able to advise on who to contact.

Discovery of archaeological sites should be dealt with in much the same way. If the site is an obvious landscape feature, it is very likely to have been recorded already. If it has been discovered during the course of earth-moving for construction or other work, however, the site may be totally unknown; in this case, it is impor-

LEFT Visiting archaeological sites is a worthwhile pursuit, particularly for those able to visit more remote and well-preserved sites. This is Machu Picchu, the 'lost' Inca city in Peru, rediscovered in 1911 by Hiram Bingham.

tant that local archaeologists are alerted as soon as possible, so that some kind of record of the site can be made before it is destroyed, or it may even be excavated if found to be important.

■ FURTHER READING

Adkins, L & Adkins RA 1982 *The Handbook of British Archaeology,* Papermac. Essential reference book for anyone interested in British archaeology; explains many terms relevant to archaeology world-wide.

Alcock, L 1971 *Arthur's Britain,* Allen Lane, The Penguin Press. Gives an insight into the problems involved in combining historical and archaeological evidence.

Barker, P 1986 *Understanding Archaeological Excavation,* Batsford. Basic introduction to some of the problems of archaeological excavation and interpretation.

Binford, LR 1983 *In Pursuit of the Past,* Thames & Hudson. Not easy to read, but does give a good insight into modern approaches to archaeological interpretation. Written by a well-known American professor of anthropology.

Carver, M 1987 *Underneath English Towns. Interpreting Urban Archaeology,* Batsford. Readable account of the techniques of interpretation and urban archaeology.

Coles, J 1973 *Archaeology by Experiment,* Scribners, New York, and Hutchinson & Co. Ltd. Readable account of archaeological experimentation.

Coles, B & Coles, J 1986 *Sweet Track to Glastonbury. The Somerset Levels in Prehistory.* Thames & Hudson. Readable, well-illustrated account of fieldwork, excavation, experiment and interpretation of prehistoric waterlogged sites.

Daniel, G 1967 *The Origins and Growth of Archaeology,* Penguin Books Ltd. Good account of the history and development of archaeology.

Daniel, G & Renfrew, C 1988 *The Idea of Prehistory,* Edinburgh University Press. Up-to-date account of the history and development of prehistoric archaeology.

Evans, JG 1978 *An Introduction to Environmental Archaeology,* Cornell University Press. Useful introduction to how archaeologists use environmental evidence.

Greene, K 1986 *The Archaeology of the Roman Economy,* Batsford. Demonstrates what can be deduced about ancient economies by combining historical and archaeological evidence.

Jackson, R 1988 *Doctors and Diseases in the Roman Empire,* British Museum Publications. Readable account of what can be achieved by combining evidence from excavations, finds, inscriptions and historical documents. Much information on ancient medical practice.

Joukowsky, M 1980 *A Complete Manual of Field Archaeology,* Prentice-Hall, Inc. Deals with many aspects of archaeology, including fieldwork and excavation.

Longworth, I & Cherry, J (eds.) 1986 *Archaeology in Britain since 1945,* British Museum Publications. Well-illustrated account of major post-war archaeological discoveries in Britain.

McIntosh, J 1986 *The Archaeologist's Handbook,* Bell & Hyman Ltd. Well-illustrated coverage of many aspects of archaeology – probably the best book to read next.

Rahtz, P 1985 *Invitation to Archaeology,* Basil Blackwell Ltd. A very readable, personal view of archaeology and archaeologists.

Reynolds, PJ 1979 *Iron-Age Farm. The Butser Experiment,* British Museum Publications. Readable, well-illustrated account of an experimental Iron Age farmstead.

Riley, DN 1987 *Air Photography & Archaeology,* Duckworth. Well-illustrated and informative account of aerial photography.

Sherratt, A (ed.) 1980 *The Cambridge Encyclopedia of Archaeology,* Cambridge University Press. Well-illustrated reference book for archaeology world-wide. Includes sections on dating and the development of archaeology.

Sklenář, K 1983 *Archaeology in Central Europe: the First 500 Years,* St. Martin's Press and Leicester University Press. The development of archaeology in Europe – complements Daniel's account.

Whitehouse, RD (ed.) 1983 *Macmillan Dictionary of Archaeology,* Macmillan Press. Good reference book for archaeology world-wide.

Woodhead, P 1985 *Keyguide to information sources in archaeology,* Mansell Publishing Limited, London and New York. Information about many aspects of archaeology world-wide, in particular organizations and publications.

OPPOSITE PAGE All archaeological sites have to be studied in relation to the surrounding landscape. Here a medieval castle is sited to take advantage of an easily defended position.

INDEX

GLOSSARY

ARCHAEOMAGNETIC DATING: it is possible to measure the orientation and intensity of the earth's magnetic field (which vary over periods of time), because it is 'preserved' or 'fossilized' in objects such as kilns which have not been moved since they were last fired. The objects can then be dated by comparison with already established sequences of dates.

CONTEXT: an individual unit of recording used in an excavation, such as a wall, ditch, layer of charcoal, cobbled surface; each context is given a unique number (context number).

DENDROCHRONOLOGY: a method of dating wood by counting annual growth rings (tree rings).

DRY SIEVING: soil is shaken through one or more sieves, so that unwanted particles pass through the mesh. The debris left in the sieve (stones and small archaeological finds) is examined, and the finds are retrieved.

FIELDWORK: all outdoor aspects of archaeology, such as survey and excavation. This term is often used more specfically to describe the searching for and plotting of sites.

FLOTATION: a method of collecting plant remains (such as seeds) by mixing soil or sediment with water in a tank; the flot (plant remains and other debris) floats and is then collected.

HAFTING: the attaching of handles (hafts) to implements, such as axes. Handles are usually made of wood and so rarely survive; the method of hafting implements in antiquity is therefore not always known.

HALF-LIFE: the time taken for half the radioactivity of a radioactive substance to disappear (decay). In radiocarbon dating, the half-life is the time taken for half the radioactivity of carbon 14 to decay (currently estimated at about 5730 years).

ISOTOPE: many elements have variants with different atomic weights, called isotopes. The most common isotope of carbon is carbon 12, but there is a radioactive isotope existing alongside it, carbon 14, which is used to measure the date of any organic item.

PALYNOLOGY: the analysis of pollen. In anaerobic and acid conditions, grains of pollen survive which can be identified and counted under a microscope, to provide an indication of the former vegetation and climate.

PETROLOGY: the examination of objects of stone and pottery to identify the minerals present, so that the source of stone or clay can be discovered. The examination is usually done by cutting a thin slice from the object (thin section) and viewing it under a microscope.

PHOTOGRAMMETRY: the science of measuring from photographs, used particularly in making maps and recording buildings. Also called stereophotogrammetry, since two cameras are used, resulting in stereo pairs of photographs which can be viewed stereoscopically, giving a three-dimensional image.

RESISTIVITY SURVEY: a method of locating buried sites by measuring the resistance of the soil to a flow of electricity using a resistivity meter. Differences in the resistance can indicate buried features of various kinds, such as ditches and walls.

SERIATION: the organization of groups of objects into a sequence, either by their appearance, or by mathemathical calculations, as a means of dating them.

SHERDS: pieces of broken pottery.

SPECTROMETRY: the identification of chemical compounds and minerals in an artefact through scientific methods which produce a spectrum of colours derived from the artefact. The variation in colours in this spectrum betrays the presence or absence of the chemical compounds and minerals.

STRATIGRAPHY: the succession of deposits laid one on top of another, so that the uppermost deposits are later in date than the lower ones. A study of the stratigraphy of the site is the basis for reconstructing its history.

TELLS: mounds formed from the build-up material (usually demolition debris from mud-brick houses) as a result of long occupation by people.

THERMOLUMINESCENCE DATING: by measuring the amount of energy released from a fired clay object (such as pottery), the length of time which has elapsed since it was last fired (usually when it was manufactured) can be measured.

TOPOGRAPHY: the study of the natural and man-made features of the landscape.

TRIREME: a classical Greek warship of the 5th–4th centuries BC, with three rows of oars on each side.

TYPOLOGY: the sorting of objects into types on the basis of similarities in form and decoration, in particular to trace variations over a period of time as a means of dating.

WET SIEVING: sediments are mixed with water, so that the unwanted particles sink. Large objects (such as stones) are collected in a sieve with a coarse mesh, while smaller organic material (such as seeds and insects) are washed off into a finer sieve and can be retrieved.

PICTURE CREDITS

930.
1
ADK

Adkins, Lesley

An introduction to
archaeology

$13.98   10/13/98